THE BEAUTY OF
Cats

CASTLE
BOOKS

THE BEAUTY OF
Cats

by Howard Loxton

Acknowledgments

Photographs were supplied by the following:

Barnaby's Picture Library: 18*l*, 19*l*, 19*r*, 23*tr*, 23*br*, 26, 31*r*, 35*tl*, 39, 41*t*, 59*bl*, 62, 63*tr*, 70*l*, 76*l*, 83*b*, 85*br*, 89*br*, 93, 97*tl*, 98*r*, 104*b*, 108*tr*, 108*br*, 109, 111*t*, 111*br*, 117*tl*, 118*l*, 118*br*, 119*l*, 131*tr*, 135*tl*, 140*l*, 142; B.P.C. Library: 121*t*; Camera Clix: 32, 49, 64*b*, 87, 95, 117*b*; Bruce Coleman: Jacket front; 42*br*, 89*cl*; C. M. Dixon: 24; Will Green: 17, 23*tl*, 27*r*, 28, 30*br*, 31*bl*, 33, 34*tr*, 36*bl*, 37*r*, 40*r*, 42*l*, 44*l*, 45*bl*, 46*b*, 48*r*, 51*tr*, 51*b*, 57*t*, 59*br*, 60*t*, 63*tl*, 63*b*, 67, 77*l*, 78*t*, 80*r*, 85*t*, 85*bl*, 88, 89*t*, 89*cr*, 94*tr*, 96, 97*tr*, 97*b*, 99, 100*t*, 101*t*, 103*tl*, 112*r*, 114, 115*t*, 116*br*, 119*r*, 122, 123*t*, 126, 127*tl*, 127*bl*, 127*r*, 129, 130*l*, 130*tr*, 131*tl*, 131*b*, 132*l*, 134*l*, 136*b*, 138*b*, 140*r*; Sonia Halliday: 81*tl*, 110*l*; Hamlyn Group/Musée Bonnat, Bayonne: 52*l*; Roy A. Harris & K. R. Duff: 10*r*, 125*r*; Michael Holford: 20*l*, 60*b*; Holyrood Amenity Trust: 47*b*; Alan Irvine: 16, 31*tl*; Bill Leimbach: 92*br*, 101*bl*; Mansell Collection: 30*tr*, 35*br*, 48*l*, 56*l*; National Film Archive: 58*tl*; National Galleries of Scotland: 46*t*; Natural History Photographic Agency: 27*l*, 34*l*, 55*b*, 79*l*, 84, 85*c*, 98*bl*, 100*bl*, 105*r*, 108*l*, 116, 128*t*, 130*br*, 135*tr*, 138*tl*, 138*tr*; Radio Times Hulton Picture Library: 30*l*, 38*tl*, 40*l*, 50, 54*l*, 64*tr*, 112*l*; Rapho: 58*tr*, 107*tr*, 107*b*, 110*r*; Snark International: 54*r*, 55*l*, 55*r*; Sotheby's: 52*r*; Spectrum Colour Library: Jacket back; 11*tl*, 11*bl*, 11*r*, 12, 13*t*, 14*t*, 15, 18*r*, 20*r*, 25, 29, 34*br*, 35*tr*, 36*br*, 37*l*, 41*b*, 42*tr*, 45*br*, 47*t*, 53, 56*l*, 57*b*, 61, 64*tl*, 71, 81*tr*, 82, 83*t*, 86*l*, 86*r*, 89*bl*, 90, 91*l*, 91*r*, 94*tl*, 94*bl*, 94*br*, 100*br*, 103*tr*, 103*b*, 111*bl*, 113, 120, 121*b*, 128*bl*, 137, 139, 143, 144; Staatliche Museen, Berlin-Dahlem: 44*r*; Syndication International: 10*l*, 13*br*, 13*bl*, 14*b*, 21, 22, 35*br*, 36*t*, 43, 51*tl*, 58*b*, 73, 81*b*, 92*l*, 92*tr*, 97*cl*, 101*br*, 102, 104*t*, 105*l*, 106*l*, 106*r*, 107*tl*, 115*bl*, 118*tr*, 125*l*, 128*br*, 132*r*, 133, 134*r*, 135*b*, 136*tr*, 141*t*, 141*lb*; Sally-Anne Thompson: 3, 68*r*, 70*r*, 75*l*, 75*r*, 77*l*, 77*r*, 78*b*, 79*r*, 124; Viewpoint Projects: 38*tr*, 38*b*, 45*t*, 68*l*, 76*r*, 80*l*, 98*tl*, 117*tr*, 123*b*, 136*tl*.

This edition published by arrangement with Trewin Copplestone Publishing Ltd.

ISBN 0 85674 000 4
Published by
Triune Press, London, England
© Trewin Copplestone Publishing Ltd 1972

Manufactured in U.S.A.

Contents

The author would like to thank Mr. K. D. Evans, M.R.C.V.S. for reading the chapters on cat health and cat care and making suggestions for their improvement.

Introduction

There are people who dislike cats, people who claim to be indifferent to them, and even people who are frightened of them—but there are few who can resist the charm of a playful kitten and surely none who can deny the beauty of the cat.

What other animal has such a graceful line and such elegant movement? Even in very long-haired cats when the body shape is softened by a mass of silky fur their luxurious appearance and lordly stride demand our admiration. Watch the ripple of muscle as a cat moves, the skill with which it stalks, the power with which it springs. When it opens its mouth we can see the terrifying teeth of the tiger but its velvet nose and gentle tongue can give the softest of caresses and its cruel claws are hidden in gentle paws. Look into a cat's deep and understanding eyes, stroke its smooth luxuriant fur and admire its richly colored coat: there is beauty here of every kind to appeal to every sense, a gentle purr, a warm, clean smell . . . and yet—that limpid gaze can turn into a calculating stare, the murderous claws unsheath, the purr change to a hissing, spitting rage. And this perhaps is the secret of the feline power. The cat has never surrendered its natural qualities or tried to come to terms with man. The hieratic power that made her worshiped, the mystery that made her feared are still present in the cat upon the hearth.

Those who have not fallen beneath her spell will call cats selfish and unfavorably compare them with the ever loyal and master-loving dog. Even cat owners will sometimes say that they prefer a cat for its independence. It is true that, on its own, a cat can manage rather better than a dog, a reflection of its later domestication. A cat is more self-reliant but as a companion it is no more self-centered than its owner. Dogs will pester for attention, cats have a natural patience.

As I write one of my own cats lies quietly outside the door guarding a piece of string and waiting for me to have the time to play with him. He may sit there for an hour without even reminding me, showing the patience his kind learned as hunters. The moment I emerge his whole frame will concentrate on that piece of string ready to spring the moment that I take it, and if I do not he will look up to show his disappointment and wait again.

To be honest, he would not be so patient if I were to forget his dinner.

His sister, younger and less restrained, may come running up, her head held high, and in her mouth a crumpled paper ball which she wants me to throw for her to retrieve. If I ignore her she will drop it at my feet and gently tap my ankle to make sure I know that it is there. If I still fail to respond she will tap my knee and plaintively ask what I am doing that is so important that I have no time to play. Having assured herself that I am at work she will not persist but either sit and watch the typewriter or be off to find some mischief she can get up to while I am too occupied to notice.

You can teach a dog a set of tricks but a cat tends to invent its own and then invite you to cooperate. Its independent resourcefulness can sometimes be too great—as on the occasion when it forces open the refrigerator door and helps itself to tomorrow's meal. Thieves and opportunists cats certainly are, but so are other animals, and man himself has not set any better example.

In his natural role of carnivorous hunters the cat has served man well. As rat catcher, mouse exterminator, snake killer, he has saved man's crops, guarded his ship's provisions, his temple manuscripts—even his life. And this has been acknowledged by putting a cat upon the payroll of many government offices and institutions from the U.S. Post Office to the British Museum.

During the Battle of Stalingrad a cat called Mourka took messages from a group of lookouts to company headquarters, during the fifteenth century a cat brought food to imprisoned Thomas Wyat, and the folk traditions of Europe have many tales which show how indebted is man to cat. Many of these stories show cats as wily schemers, even if on man's behalf, but that same cleverness makes them highly entertaining too.

Their intelligence also shows in their sensitive reaction to people's moods. They will show great concern when humans close to them are distressed and make every attempt to offer comfort. Their displays of affection are by no means limited to expressions of their own contentment. Cats will show gentleness to all those who do not harm them or form their natural prey. They are kindly toward the young of other animals, and tolerant of children, though inclined to jealousy if there is obvious competition for their owner's affection.

Above all the cat is a devoted mother. What other animal makes quite so sure that her young will be a credit to her? She will hide them from danger and fight savagely to defend them from harm. According to an old folk legend even the trees can be moved by her concern. Once upon a time, a mother cat stood distraught on the banks of a river, for her kittens had been cast in to drown. Powerless to reach them she appealed for help. So sad were her cries and so pitiful the plight of the little kittens that the riverside trees lowered their branches over the stream and trailed them in the water so that they might cling to them. In memory, each year since then the flowerless willows have decked themselves out in soft and silky buds; and those who know the story call them pussy-willows.

My Cat Jeoffry

from *Jubilate Agno* A Song from Bedlam by Christopher Smart

For I will consider my cat Jeoffry.
For he is the servant of the living God, duly and daily serving
  him.
For at the first glance of the glory of God in the East he
  worships in his way.
For is this done by wreathing his body seven times round with
  elegant quickness.
For then he leaps up to catch the musk, which is the blessing
  of God upon his prayer.
For he rolls upon prank to work in it.
For having done duty and received blessing he begins to consider
  himself.
For this he performs in ten degrees.
For first he looks upon his fore-paws to see if they are clean.
For secondly he kicks up behind to clear away there.
For thirdly he works it upon stretch with the fore-paws extended.
For fourthly he sharpens his paws by wood.
For fifthly he washes himself.
For sixthly he rolls upon wash.
For seventhly he fleas himself, that he may not be interrupted
  upon the beat.
For eighthly he rubs himself against a post.
For ninthly he looks up for his instructions.
For tenthly he goes in quest of food.
For having consider'd God and himself he will consider his
  neighbour.
For if he meets another cat he will kiss her in kindness.
For when he takes his prey he plays with it to give it a chance.
For one mouse in seven escapes by his dallying.
For when his day's work is done his business more properly
  begins.
For he keeps the Lord's watch in the night against the adversary.
For he counteracts the powers of darkness by his electrical
  skin and glaring eyes.
For he counteracts the Devil, who is death, by brisking about
  the life.
For in his morning orisons he loves the sun and the sun loves him.
For he is of the tribe of the Tiger.
For the Cherub Cat is a term of the Angel Tiger.
For he has the subtlety and hissing of a serpent, which in
  goodness he suppresses.
For he will not do destruction, if he is well-fed, neither
  will he spit without provocation.
For he purrs in thankfulness, when God tells him he's a good
  Cat.
For he is an instrument for the children to learn benevolence
  upon.

For every house in incompleat without him & a blessing is
lacking in the spirit.
For the Lord commanded Moses concerning the cats at the depart-
ure of the Children of Israel from Egypt.
For every family had one cat at least in the bag.
For the English cats are the best in Europe.
For he is the cleanest in the use of his fore-paws of any
quadrupede.
For the dexterity of his defence is an instance of the love of
God to him exceedingly.
For he is the quickest to his mark of any creature.
For he is tenacious of his point.
For he is a mixture of gravity and waggery.
For he knows that God is his Saviour.
For there is nothing sweeter than his peace when at rest.
For there is nothing brisker than his life when in motion.
For he is of the Lord's poor and so indeed is he called by
benevolence perpetually—Poor Jeoffry! poor Jeoffry! the rat
has bit thy throat.
For I bless the name of the Lord Jesus that Jeoffry is better.
For the divine spirit comes about his body to sustain it in
compleat cat.
For his tongue is exceeding pure so that it has in purity what
it wants in musick.
For he is docile and can learn certain things.
For he can set up with gravity which is patience upon approbation.
For he can fetch and carry, which is patience in employment.
For he can jump over a stick which is patience upon proof positive.
For he can spraggle upon waggle at the word of command.
For he can jump from an eminence into his master's bosom.
For he can catch the cork and toss it again.
For he is hated by the hypocrite and miser.
For the former is afraid of detection.
For the latter refused the charge.
For he camels his back to bear the first motion of business.
For he is good to think on, if a man would express himself neatly.
For he made a great figure in Egypt for his signal services.
For he killed the Icneumon-rat very pernicious by land.
For his ears are so acute that they sting again.
For from this proceeds the passing quickness of his attention.
For by stroaking of him I have found out electricity.
For I perceived God's light about him both wax and fire.
For the Electrical fire is the spiritual substance,
which God sends from heaven to sustain the bodies
both of man and beast.
For God has blessed him in the variety of his movements.
For, tho he cannot fly, he is an excellent clamberer.
For his motions upon the face of the earth are more
than any other quadrupede.
For he can tread to all the measures upon the musick.
For he can swim for life.
For he can creep.

The Cat Family

Many so-called wild cats are really domestic cats which have become feral, like the one above. One of the true wild cats is the European wildcat (*Felis silvestris*), one of the species from which the domestic cat developed.

The cat family includes a wide range of animals from the lion to the domestic cat. They all have the same kind of skeleton, fur, whiskers, paw pads and retractile claws. Zoologists divide them into two main subfamilies depending on the development of a series of bones at the base of the tongue. In the *Panthera* one of the bones has developed only as a thread-like ligament and these animals, which include the larger cats—the lion, tiger, leopard, snow leopard, clouded leopard and jaguar—can roar but cannot purr. They also have round pupils to their eyes. The *Felis* group can purr but not roar and usually have vertical pupils. They include the puma, jaguarundi, ocelot, margay, serval, lynx, golden cat and a number of small wildcats as well as our house cat. The cheetah, whose claws are only partly retractile, is given a genus to itself—*Acinonyx*.

None of the cats are native to Australia, New Zealand, the islands of Oceania, Madagascar or the West Indies, and only one, the lynx, is found both in the Old World and the Americas. The jaguar is the only New World *Panthera* but the puma, ocelot, jaguarundi, Margay and bobcat are all American cats—though none of them reached South America until comparatively recent times, about one million years ago, when the Panama land-bridge was reestablished in the course of the movements of the continents.

The early cat was in existence long before that. It probably developed about fifty million years ago from a weasel-like meat eater which carried its long body around on little legs. It has been given the scientific name *Miacis* and is also believed to have been the ancestor of the dog, the bear and the civet. Its evolution, first into a civet-like animal and then into a cat, took about ten million years, which is extremely rapid in evolutionary terms—less than half the time it took for the dog family to develop.

This first cat, known as *Dinictis*, was about the size of a lynx. It must have been very well adapted to its environment for it remained largely unchanged at a time when other mammals were developing rapidly. *Dictinis* had much larger canine teeth than modern cats and from it developed, in one direction, the now extinct saber-toothed tiger whose bones have been preserved in their hundreds in the La Brea tar beds of San Francisco, and in the other the smaller-toothed wildcat whose bones show that eight million years ago it was very similar to the wildcats of today. The physical differences between modern wildcats and domestic cats are largely a matter of size and fur length and the hard protective pads of the wildcat's paws. Their similarities are so great that it is difficult to establish the later genealogy of the house cat with any certainty.

An ocelot **(above)**, a cheetah and a cheetah cub. Members of the cat family have many common characteristics: they walk upon their toes, which makes them silent hunters, have sensitive whiskers, sharp eyes, acute hearing and tongues with a rasp-like surface.

How the cat became domesticated is a matter of conjecture, though the folk stories of the world offer many suggestions. The Khasi people of Assam, for instance, tell how the cat lived happily with her brother the tiger until one day the tiger began to shiver and shake. When the tiger got no better and seemed to tremble all over with the cold the cat decided that she must go in search of fire to warm him.

Only man had fire so that cat went to his house. There was no answer when she called so she went in. The fire was burning brightly on the hearth and since there was no one to ask she was about to carry some away when she noticed a dish of rice and some fish set out on the floor. They smelled good, they looked good, they were delicious. Her stomach full, and feeling drowsy from the warmth, she fell asleep beside the hearth.

The cat seemed to have been away for ages and tiger wondered what had happened to her. He gathered all his failing strength and called. At last the cat heard him. Stirring guiltily, she took a burning brand in her mouth and ran back to him. But her fireside sleep had been very pleasant and the rice and fish much to her taste. Life with man would be much more comfortable than life in the wild so she told her brother that was how she planned to live in future and ran back to the house.

It seems likely that it was the cat who chose to live with man rather than man who set out deliberately to capture and domesticate the cat. And that still remains the basic cat-human relationship.

When the cat was first domesticated we cannot be sure. In Switzerland cat bones have been found in association with prehistoric men but since the bones of other wild carnivores were present it is unlikely that there were domesticated cats. A cat of about 2000 BC found in the Indus Valley may have been domesticated, but the evidence is disputable and most authorities suggest that the Egyptians were the first to domesticate the cat. There are no known representations of cats in the cave paintings of prehistoric man; the earliest known was painted about 2600 B.C. in an Egyptian tomb of the Fifth Dynasty. It shows a cat wearing a wide collar but it could be a wildcat, for although a cat cult was probably established in Egypt before 2000 BC the earliest undisputed date for a domestic cat is about 1600 BC. From then on there are frequent representations of domestic cats in Egyptian art.

Other members of the cat family include the cheetah **(opposite)**, the leopard **(top)**, the puma **(right)** and the caracal lynx. The big cats and their smaller relations display a wide variety of coat patterns which provide excellent camouflage in the wild.

It is generally agreed that the Egyptian house cats developed from the African wildcat, *Felis lybica*, to give its scientific name. *Lybica*, and the European wildcat *Felis silvestris*, are the only wild members of the *Felis* family to have the familiar striped tabby markings which form the only coat pattern common for domestic cats throughout the world. All the Egyptian cats appear to have been tabbies and they may originally have been domesticated wildcats or, since they were larger than the wildcat, they could have been a cross between it and the larger African jungle cat, *Felis chaus*, or one of its subspecies (though not tabbies). *Felis chaus* takes its name from the original meaning of jungle—hot, dry scrubland, like its habitat. Mummified remains have shown that the skulls of the Egyptian cats were larger than those of modern cats.

Since the Egyptians tried to prevent the export of their cats which were considered extremely valuable by the Romans, there must have been a clear difference between wild and domestic species, for no value was placed on the wildcats of Europe.

The lion **(above)**, tiger **(right)** and Chinese leopard (cub), **(left)** belong to the *Panthera* group of cats and are not so closely related to the domestic cat as are the *Felis* family. Unlike the other cats the adult male develops a long mane and has a tufted tip to its tail. Lion cubs have spots and stripes on their coat like other cats but these fade as they grow older.

Experts differ as to whether all modern domestic cats owe their origin to those of ancient Egypt. Other wildcats have probably played their part. Unlike the easily tamed *lybica*, *silvestris* is virtually untameable, but the spotted yellow desert cat of India can be easily tamed if taken as a kitten. In America both ocelots and margays have been kept as pets. The cheetah, too, can be domesticated and trained. In Egypt, India and other parts of Asia, it has been used as hunter and retriever; it has been used to kill coyotes in the United States. It has also been claimed that the Indians of Paraguay domesticated the jaguarundi before Columbus sailed across the Atlantic. If you should be tempted to keep one of these exotic animals as a pet remember that they *are* wild and will need very careful handling. You should also make sure that you are within the law, since there is legislation in some American cities which forbids the keeping of wild animals, though it may be possible for a lawyer to prove that your pet is truly domesticated and no longer wild.

The Sacred Cat

'Praise to thee, O Ra, . . .

thou art the Great Cat, the avenger of the Gods'

Ancient Egyptians carved that song of praise more than three thousand years ago at the entrance to the royal tombs in the Valley of the Kings, near Thebes. It is one of the 'Litanies of the Sun', seventy-five different ways of praising the sun god Ra, creator and ruler of the world. In two papyri in the British Museum there are pictures of Ra the great cat slaying his arch-enemy Apep, the serpent of darkness. The serpent, like Ra, is immortal and must be vanquished again each morning. In another papyrus, one of the Books of the Dead, which are a kind of guide book for the journey to, and life in, the afterworld, we can read: 'I am the Cat which fought hard by the Persea Tree in Heliopolis on the night when the foes of Neb-er-tcher were destroyed.'

Who is this cat?

This male cat is Ra himself and he was called Mau because of the word of the god Sa, who said of him: 'He is like unto that which he hath made; therefore did the name of Ra become Mau.'

Mau, as you may guess from the sound, was the Egyptian word for cat. The Persea Tree, like the tree in the Garden of Eden, was a tree of life and knowledge. When there was an eclipse of the sun the 'great cat's' victory was in doubt; sometimes the serpent was believed even to have swallowed the boat in which Ra sailed. Then the Egyptians shook the rattle-like instruments called sistra, which usually carried the head or figure of a cat, to encourage the god in his struggle with the powers of darkness. Both cats and snakes, when they lie, coil themselves into a circle, and are therefore natural symbols of eternity. Natural too is the struggle between them, for cats are fascinated by snakes and one of the animals capable of overcoming them, though there is little evidence that they ever eat them.

The game called 'Cat's Cradle' which children play with string links the cat with the sun god in other cultures. In the Congo the game was used to encourage the sun to rest when he was parching the earth, while Eskimos played it to trap the sun and prevent the winter darkness.

The 'great cat' was only one of the many manifestations of Ra. The first of the true cat deities was the goddess Mafdet. In the pyramid texts, magic formulas to protect the Pharaoh in the next world which were carved on the walls of pyramid chambers of the Fifth and Sixth Dynasties (before 2280 BC), she is presented as a snake-killing cat, the protectress of Pharaoh in the royal palace. Perhaps the goddess was identified with a real cat who protected the Pharaoh's home. But there is no indication that cats were actually domesticated by this time, although wildcats appear in paintings in the tombs of the Old Kingdom which depict the wild life of the marshes.

16

Protective amulets in the shape of cats or cats' heads, and magical wands engraved with cats—some of them holding knives or destroying snakes, as Mau-Ra and Mafdet did—suggest some kind of cat cult as early as the Sixth Dynasty. At Abydos in a tomb of the Twelfth Dynasty, Sir Flinders Petrie discovered 'seventeen skeletons of cats and, in the offering recess, a row of the roughest little offering pots'. The offerings, presumably of milk, would have been magically replenished by the ministrations of the priests.

By the Seventeenth Dynasty cats had found royal favor and appear on the golden bracelets of King Antef; the number of amulets and scarabs with cat figures greatly increased. Sometimes the scarabs link the cat with the name of Bast, an Egyptian goddess who, in the confusing way that Egyptian deities seemed to be many things at the same time, was the daughter and the spouse of the sun god, the wife of Ptah, the Lady of Life, the Soul of Osiris and the Eye of Ra. In Egyptian, mau, name of Ra—and word for cat—also means to see.

Bast (or Bastet or Pasht) was originally a lion-headed goddess, and at Bubastis, in Lower Egypt, the center of her cult, the lion-headed form persisted. She personified the fertilizing warmth of the sun. In later times she was usually depicted as a cat-headed woman. A goddess of love and pleasure, she enjoyed music and the dance and is shown holding a sistrum. She was originally the protector goddess of the Bubastis region but when about 950 BC the Libyan Pharaohs made Bubastis the capital of the kingdom, she became a national goddess and seems to have absorbed all lesser cat deities. Even today, the mound that marks the site of Bubastis has the Arab name Tell-Basta.

Another lion-headed goddess, known as Sekhmet, was closely linked, and often confused, with Bast. Both were worshiped in the Temple of the Sun at Heliopolis where Sekhmet, the Big Cat, represented the very hot, destructive aspect of the sun and Bast, the Little Cat, its fruitful, life-giving power: 'Kindly she is as Bast, terrible as Sekhmet,' the Egyptians said. Bast became one of the most popular goddesses and her sacred animal, the cat, one of the most venerated.

Bast was worshiped at Bubastis as early as the Twelfth Dynasty (before 1780 BC). Her popularity was undiminished until the suppression of paganism by the Byzantine emperor Theodosius I in AD 392. The cult flourished for longer than the Christian Church has so far existed.

The Greek historian Herodotus, who visited Egypt in 450 BC, wrote of the temple at Bubastis: 'Other temples may be grander, and may have cost more in building, but there is none so pleasant to the eye.' In the courtyard of the temple lived the shrine's own cats which the priests would watch carefully for any message from the goddess. The care of the sacred animals was a special honor which descended from father to son. When an Egyptian wished to make a vow to the goddess he would partly shave the head of his child—the proportion of shaving presumably depending on the kind of vow—and weigh the clippings against silver. 'And whatever sum the hair weighs is presented to the guardian of the animals, who thereupon cuts up some fish, and gives it to them for food.'

Herodotus goes on to recount two very strange tales about the Egyptian cats:

The number of domestic animals in Egypt is very great, and would be still greater were it not for what befalls the cats. As the females, when they have kittened, no longer seek the company of the males, these last, to obtain once more their companionship, practise a curious artifice. They seize the kittens, carry them off, and kill them, but do not eat them afterwards. Upon this the females, being deprived of their young, and longing to supply their place, seek the males once more, since they are particularly fond of their offspring. On every occasion of a fire in Egypt the strangest prodigy occurs with the cats. The inhabitants allow the fire to rage as it pleases, while they stand about at intervals and watch these animals, which, slipping by the men or else leaping over them, rush headlong into the flames. When this happens, the Egyptians are in deep affliction. If a cat dies in a private house by a natural death, all the inmates of the house shave their eyebrows.

The cat-headed goddess Bast. In her right hand she holds a sistrum, a rattle-like instrument, and in her left the aegis, a small basket.

The Egyptians grew to love their domestic cats as much as they venerated them as sacred animals. Their pets appear, ready to perpetuate their companionship in the underworld, in wall paintings and carvings of tombs from the sixteenth century BC. At Thebes, in the tomb of the sculptor Api, a painting of about 1400 BC shows a playful kitten on his knee while beneath his wife's chair sits her pet with a silver ring in its ear. In another Theban tomb of about the same date a cat with a pink tongue and a long tail was painted sitting beneath a lady's chair at a feast; dating from some sixty years earlier is the pet cat of a harbormaster's wife shown tethered to a chair leg by a leash, trying to detach the ribbon with a paw so that she can reach a bowl of food. The back of the throne of Queen Thyi, mother of the Pharaoh Akhenaton (ruled 1379–1361 BC), which is now in Cairo Museum, shows her sitting in a narrow pleasure boat with her pet cat beneath her chair. A similar cat appears eating a goose beneath the chair of her brother in his tomb at Thebes. There the head has been defaced. Akhenaton tried to introduce a monotheistic religion; but when the old gods were reinstated the cat may have been seen as a representative of the one god and its head deliberately erased, as were the representations of the god in Akhenaton's capital at Tell el Amarna.

The Egyptians taught their cats to act as retrievers when they went hunting in the marshes of the Delta. A wall painting from the tomb of Nebamen at Thebes (c. 1400 BC) assures him **that** there will be hunting cats in his after-life.

In the sanctuaries of their gods the Egyptians fed animals whom they thought to be the god in physical form: a bull for Ptah, a crocodile for Sebek, a falcon for Horus, an ibis for Thoth—and a cat for Bast. These animals were so much venerated that throughout the province which each god protected all animals of his or her particular species were considered sacred. It was forbidden to eat them and to kill them was a terrible crime punishable by death. Since this rule held only for each god's province, it was the cause of inter-provincial strife. However the cat became so important that it was revered all over Egypt.

According to Herodotus, a man had to die even for accidentally killing an ibis or a hawk, whereas for a cat he was let off with a fine. Nevertheless such was the strength of popular feeling that Diodorus Siculus, four centuries later, observed that even someone who accidentally killed a cat was likely to be lynched, so that if an Egyptian saw one lying dead he would hurry away wailing his grief and trying to prove by his protestations that he had nothing to do with its death.

During the first century BC, Cleopatra's father Ptolemy Auletes negotiated a peace treaty with Rome. 'The Roman Ambassadors,' so Edward Topsell retold the story, after Diodorus, 'remaining still in Egypt, it fortuned that a Roman unawares killed a Cat, which being by the multitude of the Egyptians espied, they presently fell upon the Ambassador's house, to rase down the same, except the offender might be delivered unto them to suffer death: so that

neither the honour of the Roman name, nor the necessity of peace, could have restrained them from that fury, had not the King himself and his greatest lords come in person, not so much to deliver the Roman cat-murderer, as to safeguard him from the people's violence.'

Both temple cats and domestic pets were accorded the funeral rites of Egypt, as were other sacred animals. They were mummified and encased and often buried with food which was renewed through the incantations of the priests. Kittens would be simply dipped into a solution of preservative chemicals and then wrapped in linen. Consequently their remains have survived only as bundles of dust and fragmented bones. Adult cats were more elaborately preserved. Treated with chemicals, oils and spices, they were carefully and—if the owner was rich—elaborately wrapped. The body was arranged with the rear legs brought up in a sitting posture, the front paws stretched straight down and the tail brought forward to lie against the belly. After winding it in a sheet of linen it was wrapped in a cylindrical covering of plaited ribbons in two colors, possibly intended to suggest the original markings of the coat. A papier-mâché mask covered the head, with colored linen disks sewn on to represent the eyes and nostrils and pieces of palm leaves shaped to form the alert and upright ears.

The mummy was then placed inside a mummy case or a funerary box, which might be of wood or bronze, and was usually in the shape of a seated cat. The wooden cases were often painted and sometimes had bronze heads, or had the heads painted to suggest metal. One in the British Museum has a body painted white to represent bandages and a green-painted head. Some human mummy cases also carry portraits with green faces but the significance is not clear. Perhaps the color simply represents a metallic face mask.

Kittens in particular might be placed in a small bronze box, probably surmounted by a statue of a cat. In the Langton Collection there is one only three inches long which must have been made for an almost new-born kitten. It is guarded by the figures of four bronze kittens.

Herodotus believed that all cats were sent to Bubastis for burial but cat burials have been found at many other sites. Nevertheless, many cats *were* sent there and nineteenth-century Egyptologists discovered a mass cemetery with more than 300,000 embalmed and mummified cats laid upon tiered shelves in subterranean tunnels. At the time no one seemed to care very much about them. Their heads were slashed off and the contents spread upon the earth to manure the local crops. Twenty tons were shipped from Alexandria to England, pulverized, and sold as fertilizer at a price of four pounds sterling (ten dollars) per ton. Meanwhile, in all the museums of the world, only a handful of cat mummies survived, or so it was believed until, in 1952, an unopened crate was discovered in the vaults of the British Museum which had been brought back from Egypt half a century before. Its contents came from Giza and consisted of 192 mummified cats, 7 mongooses, 3 dogs and a fox, which are thought to date 600–200 BC. Of the cats, four are *Felis chaus*, and the rest seem to represent a halfway stage between the African wildcat and the modern domestic cat.

A mosaic of the second century A.D. from Rome. A very similar mosaic was found at Pompeii. One Roman writer recommended that cats be kept not only as a protection against mice but to keep small rodents out of the garden. Romans prized the cats of Egypt very highly and some Romans even adopted the Egyptian cult of cat worship.

The Egyptians were very jealous of their pets. Their attitude was known to their contemporaries. A comic poet from Rhodes has a character comment to an Egyptian: 'If you see a sick cat you weep for it. As far as I'm concerned, I'll happily kill it for its skin.' Plutarch describes the care with which the Egyptians mate their females to a male whose character is compatible with hers.

In 500 BC the Persian king Cambyses was besieging Pelusium, near where Port Said stands today, and meeting fierce resistance from the Egyptians. Knowing how the Egyptians venerated cats he ordered his soldiers to scour the countryside for them. When they had gathered all they could, he gave the order for them to advance upon the town. Each soldier carried a cat, like a shield, before him, and in front of the army they drove all the other cats. The devout men of Pelusium could not strike a blow to defend themselves against the attack without endangering the lives of the sacred cats. Pelusium surrendered without a blow being struck.

Although the export of cats was prohibited some did leave Egypt. Phoenician traders, who sailed the length and breadth of the Mediterranean and to such distant lands as Britain, smuggled them out and sold them.

The Greeks do not seem to have given them much attention, though they appear in one or two vase paintings, in a relief and on two coins of Tarentum. Diodorus Siculus, the first-century Sicilian, who was amused to see the Egyptians crumbling bread into milk and cutting up fish for their cats, wrote of a birdless mountain in Numidia (approximately modern Algeria) which was inhabited by a whole commonwealth of cats; it was supposed that hunters captured them and carried them to Greece.

In the time of the emperors, when exotic religions became a fashionable fad, some Romans took up cat worship like the Egyptians. At Portici, near Mount Vesuvius, two paintings were discovered which show a priest of Isis, and a woman kneeling and holding a sistrum. They appear to be worshiping a cat sitting on an outsize sistrum. Isis, the Egyptian goddess who was wife and sister of Osiris, is sometimes given a cat emblem but the sistrum was particularly linked with Bast. When a temple to the Goddess of Liberty was built in Rome in the second century BC a cat was depicted at the foot of her statue and became a symbol of freedom for the Romans.

In more ordinary circumstances, the cat would be thought of as an exotic and useful pet. At Pompeii, a woman was found entombed in the solidified lava with a cat in her arms and in the House of the Faun a mosaic shows a less lovable cat carrying off a chicken. In late Roman times in a treatise on agriculture, Palladius recommended the keeping of cats to protect gardens from mice and moles. Cats must have been known throughout the Empire. Figurines have been found at settlements in France and Spain and a number of cat skeletons have been discovered on Roman sites in Britain.

The 'Familiar' Cat

The Greeks and Romans identified the Egyptian goddess Bast, the cat of the sun, with Diana or Artemis, the Greek and Roman goddesses of the moon. The transition is not so strange as first appears for both are sisters of the sun god, Bast of Ra and Artemis of Apollo. The fecundity of the cat is in contrast to the virginity of Artemis, yet Diana's name was also given to the great fertility goddess Diana of Ephesus. Cats love warmth and the sun but equally they are nocturnal animals and it seems natural to link them with the moon. They like to curl up at the fireside—and fire and light and linked in the Roman goddess Vesta, who was served by virgin priestesses. In the overlapping of attributes between the ancient deities there are many occasions when their influence extends over apparently contradictory fields.

Deities with similar attributes appear in the pantheons of many lands. Chinese farmers, for instance, used to worship a cat god called Li Shou and at the end of the harvest held an orgiastic festival which included sacrificial offerings to the cats which had kept rodents from the corn. The Machica Indians of Peru also had a feline deity, often depicted as a man with cat's whiskers, who was the god of copulation.

The cat's position as a fertility figure accounts for it being the sacrifice itself in the once widespread custom of killing a cat as the last sheaf of corn was reaped. In eastern Europe a cat was buried alive in a field of corn to ensure a good harvest and in part of France a kitten buried in the ground was thought to prevent the growth of weeds. In *The Golden Bough* Sir James Frazer describes how in France and Germany well-fed cats were garlanded with flowers and

The nocturnal habits of the cat were one reason why superstitious people used to associate it with the devil, either as his servant or as a shape in which Satan himself would appear. The sudden appearance of a cat's eyes shining out of the darkness can still be very frightening and its swift and silent approach could easily suggest the arrival of a spirit.

ritually eaten on the first day of the harvest. In Aix-en-Provence during the Middle Ages, the Church supported a loosely Christianized ceremony in which on each Corpus Christi Day a tomcat was displayed wrapped like a baby in tight swaddling bands, then, at exactly noon, publicly burned. It is difficult to see how the priests linked Jesus with this pagan ceremony which obviously had its origin in sun-worship—can the cat have been proxy for Christ himself? These ritual sacrifices, like the actual or symbolic sacrifice of a priest or king which features in almost all religions and folk cultures, gave the cat a place of honor. But, for the most part, as Christianity spread, the cat's association with Diana and with the night made it a symbol of the devil, for Diana became Hecate, the queen of the night and chief of the witches. There are similarities with the Nordic Freya, who traveled in a chariot drawn by a pair of cats. There was a revival of her cult in the fifteenth century when, Hecate-like, she was linked with another goddess, Holda, who had a retinue of virgins who either rode on or disguised themselves as cats to attend frenzied orgies presided over by the devil.

   In France, particularly, peasants believed that cats, especially black ones, had a close link with the devil. *L'Evangile du Diable* (*The Devil's Bible*) declares 'Only fools do not know that all cats have a pact with the Devil. . . . It is clear why cats sleep, or feign sleep, all day long, by the fire in winter or in the sun in summer. Their task is to keep watch in the barns and stables through the night, to see all, to hear all. It is easy to see why the Evil Spirits, warned just in time, always manage to disappear before we can see them.'

A black cat was also one of the forms in which the devil himself might appear. In the twelfth and thirteenth centuries the Waldensians and Albigensians, who were persecuted and massacred as heretics, were accused of rites involving cats. When Pope Clement V suppressed the order of Knights Templar at the beginning of the fourteenth century its members confessed under torture that they had worshiped the devil in the form of a black tomcat. In these superstitious times fear and prejudice led to the persecution of both cat and cat-lover.

In 1344 there was an outbreak of St Vitus' Dance in the French town of Metz. A knight arrived at the peak of the epidemic and took lodgings in the town. When he was about to fall asleep he saw an enormous black cat sitting on the hearth staring at him. No sooner had he made the sign of the cross and drawn his sword than the cat disappeared leaving only the sound of hissed blasphemies behind. Next day not a citizen twitched or pranced; the epidemic was over. The knight was convinced that the cat had been the devil and the city authorities agreed. They organized a public burning of cats and each year for more than four hundred years thereafter the people of Metz ceremonially burned thirteen cats who were imprisoned in an iron cage and set on the top of a great bonfire built on the esplanade. In Paris and in other European towns similar ceremonies have been recorded. No doubt the Church had taken over the still surviving pagan sacrifice and reversed its symbolism to make it a Christian ceremony.

At the coronation of Elizabeth I, in 1559, English Protestants carried in procession a wicker effigy of the pope which was finally burned on a pyre. Inside the wicker cage were live cats who 'squalled in a most hideous manner as soon as they felt the fire,' cries which were described as 'the language of the devils within the body of the Holy Father'.

28

In England and Scotland toward the end of Elizabeth's reign and at the beginning of that of her successor, James I, there was a burst of interest in, and prosecution of, witches. James, who was already king of Scotland, personally interrogated accused witches at his Edinburgh palace of Holyrood House. One group confessed that the Earl of Bothwell had asked them to contrive the king's death. Agnes Tompson told how 'at the time His Majesty was in Denmark she . . . took a cat and christened it, and afterward bound to each part of that cat the chiefest parts of a dead man, and several joints of his body; and that in the night following, the said cat was conveyed in their riddles or sieves . . . and so left the said cat right before the town of Leith in Scotland. This done, there did arise such a tempest in the sea as a greater hath not been seen; which tempest was the cause of perishing of a boat or vessel coming . . . to the town of Leith. . . . And further, the said witch declared, his Majesty had never come safely from the sea if his faith had not prevailed above their intentions.'

King James became fascinated by witches and wrote a book about them called *Daemonologie*. His interest may have encouraged a greater number of prosecutions but his many investigations seem to have undermined his own belief in the supernatural or at least to have made

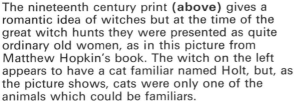

The nineteenth century print (above) gives a romantic idea of witches but at the time of the great witch hunts they were presented as quite ordinary old women, as in this picture from Matthew Hopkin's book. The witch on the left appears to have a cat familiar named Holt, but, as the picture shows, cats were only one of the animals which could be familiars.

him eager to expose counterfeit bewitchment and prevent supposed witches being prosecuted. Nevertheless William Shakespeare, to please him, wrote *Macbeth*. In this play the good character Banquo is actually one of James' ancestors, and there are also the famous witches, one of whom had a 'familiar' in the form of a brindled (or streaked) cat called Graymalkin.

The animal familiar seems to have been a particularly English phenomenon. Elsewhere, a witch may occasionally have, as in the Faust stories, a supernatural 'servant' who doubles as a keeper to make sure the damned does not slip out of the devil's grasp. But the usual link with demons is with a devil lover and animals play their part only as an ingredient in spells. Whilst continental witches were often thought to have the power to turn themselves into animals, British witches had a magical servant to run their errands and carry out their wishes. The servant, or familiar, might take all kinds of shapes and a cat was by no means the most common, but it is the form which has stayed strongest in the popular imagination. Anyone who has lived with a cat knows the strange interdependence of owner and pet, and in an age when ordinary folk had little time to waste on animals it must have been easy to imagine a more sinister relationship between a lonely old woman and her feline companion. There are many examples in reports of witch trials.

In 1582, eight-year-old Thomas Rabbet of St. Osyth in Essex gave evidence that his mother had 'four several spirits, the one called Tiffin, the other Titty, the third Piggin, and the fourth

Jack, and being asked of what colours they were, sith that Titty is like a little grey cat, Tiffin is like a white lamb, Piggin is black, like a toad, and Jack is black, like a cat. And he saith, he hath seen his mother at times to give them beer to drink, and of a white loaf or cake to eat; and saith that in the night-time she said spirits will come to his mother and suck blood of her upon her arms and other places of her body.'

In 1618 Ellen Green, a Leicestershire witch, told in her confession how another witch, called Joan Willimot, had come to her and persuaded her 'to forsake God and betake her to the Devil, and she would give her two spirits, to which she gave her consent; and thereupon . . . called two spirits, one in the likeness of a kitlin [kitten] and the other of a moldiwarp [mole]. The first the said Willimot called "Puss!", the other "Hiss, hiss!", and they presently came to her, and she departing left them with this examinate; and they leaped on her shoulder, and the kitlin sucked under her right ear on her neck and the moldiwarp on the left side in the like place. After they had sucked her, she sent the kitlin to a baker . . . who had called her "Witch" and stricken her, and bade her said spirit go and bewitch him to death.'

This idea of familiars being suckled by the witch or drinking their blood, vampire-like, was well established. People even believed that witches had an extra nipple for their familiars. Since many cats delight in sleeping on their owners' beds and even creeping under the covers, it is not difficult to see how a malicious mind could invent all kinds of horrors.

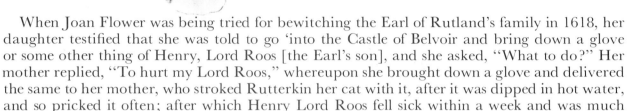

When Joan Flower was being tried for bewitching the Earl of Rutland's family in 1618, her daughter testified that she was told to go 'into the Castle of Belvoir and bring down a glove or some other thing of Henry, Lord Roos [the Earl's son], and she asked, "What to do?" Her mother replied, "To hurt my Lord Roos," whereupon she brought down a glove and delivered the same to her mother, who stroked Rutterkin her cat with it, after it was dipped in hot water, and so pricked it often; after which Henry Lord Roos fell sick within a week and was much tormented with the same.

'She further saith, that finding a glove about two or three years since of Francis, Lord Roos, on a dunghill, she delivered it to her mother, who put it into hot water and after took it out and rubbed it on Rutterkin the cat and bade him go upwards [lie on his back], and after, her mother buried it in the yard and said, "A mischief light on him! but he will mind again."'

Joan Flower used a similar kind of spell to prevent the Countess having further children but when she tried to bewitch the Earl's daughter Katherine by rubbing a piece of her handkerchief on the cat's belly 'Rutterkin whined and cried "Mew!", whereupon she said that Rutterkin had no power over the Lady Katherine to hurt her.'

Contemporary pamphlets and trial records tell many similar stories, though not all of them resulted in death for the witches. The powerful Fairfax family of Yorkshire failed to obtain the conviction of a company of witches for bewitching their children, despite detailed evidence which included the declaration that one of them, Jennet Dibble, had an attendant spirit 'in the shape of a great black cat called Gibbe, which hath attended her now above forty years'. A long life-span for a household pet!

Contrary to the usual English practice, the self-appointed Witch Finder General of England, Matthew Hopkins, used torture to extract confessions and in 1645–6 sent more than two hundred witches to their end. Despite the savage persecution there were sceptics like the Puritan parson John Gaule who published a collection of sermons on witchcraft in 1646 in which he declared that 'Every old woman with a wrinkled face, a hairy lip, a squint eye, a spindle in her hand, and a cat or dog by her side, is not only suspected but pronounced for a witch.'

Witch persecution crossed the Atlantic to the New World where its most famous outbreak was at Salem, Massachusetts, in 1692. Cotton Mather, the Puritan preacher whose book on the occult helped to spark off the hysteria, though he himself was sceptical of the evidence in many cases, recorded the testimony of Robert Downer at the trial of Susanna Martin on 29 June 1692. Downer informed the court that when the defendant had been prosecuted some years before he had told her that he believed she was a witch. She had then threatened him 'That some she-devil would shortly fetch him away.' The following night when he was in bed 'There came in at the Window the likeness of a Cat, which fell upon him, took fast hold of

In Britain and Europe black cats are considered lucky, in America white ones, and in the east tortoiseshells bring luck.

his Throat, lay on him a considerable while, and almost killed him.' He remembered Susanna Martin's threat and cried out 'Avoid, Thou She-Devil! In the Name of God the Father, the Son, and the Holy Ghost, Avoid! whereupon it left him, leap'd on the Floor, and flew out at the Window.'

Most witches were brought to trial when someone who believed they had suffered from their magic accused them, but in 1662 Isobel Gowdie of Morayshire in Scotland voluntarily went to the authorities and gave one of the most detailed confessions on record that she was a witch, something not even her own husband had suspected. She claimed to have the power to change her shape and gave the following spells for turning into a cat and back again:

> *I shall goe intill ane catt,*
> *With sorrow, and sych, and a blak shott;*
> *And I shall goe in the Divellis nam,*
> *Ay guhill I com hom againe.*

To turn back again she had to say:

> *Catt, catt, God send the a blak shott,*
> *I am in a cattis likness just now,*
> *But I sal be in a womanis liknes ewin now.*
> *Catt, catt, God send thee a blak shott.*

The folklore of the world is full of stories of women who turn into cats. Usually they are surprised in their cat form or attack someone who then wounds or mutilates them in some easily recognizable way, as in a Norwegian story of a miller whose mill had twice been burned down on the eve of Whit Sunday. On the anniversary the following year he kept watch, taking care to draw a magic circle around himself as a protection from evil. To his amazement he saw a band of cats creep into the mill bearing a pot full of pitch. They lit a fire beneath the pot and began to swing it backwards and forwards. Before the cats could spill the molten pitch into the fire and set the mill aflame the miller shouted to them from the safety of the magic circle. The witches stopped and their leader tried to pull him out of the safety of the circle. The miller drew his knife and cut off the witch cat's paw and the coven fled; the mill was saved. Imagine the miller's horror when, next morning, he discovered that his own wife's hand had been severed at the wrist.

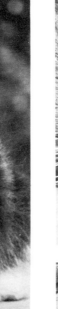

This woodcut of three witches comes from a seventeenth-century broadsheet reporting their trial. They were Anne Baker, Joan Willimot and Ellen Green who were all linked with the case of Joan Flower in 1618. Ellen said that Joan Willimot gave her two spirits called Puss and Hiss.

An American version of the story, told in the Ozark Mountains, features a braggart who took on a wager to sleep in a house where witches were supposed to meet. With a bottle of whisky to keep him company he waited till midnight and nothing happened. Then, just as he was about to fall asleep, an enormous cat appeared howling and spitting. The drunkard drew his pistol and fired at his attacker. As the shot rang out he heard a woman's scream and his candle was knocked over, leaving him in darkness, but as the flame guttered out he thought he saw a bare and bloody foot. In the morning there was nothing to be seen but he was told that a woman who lived close by had accidentally shot her foot off and died from loss of blood.

There are stories of wives who turn into cats to steal out at night and visit their lovers. There are stories of cats who are so enamored of young men that they turn into women to become their lovers. Aesop tells a fable about this: a mouse scampering across the bedroom so rouses all the cat's instincts that she leaps from her lover's bed to chase it across the floor.

From Japan comes the story of the vampire cat of Nabeshima: The Prince of Hizen had a favorite lady known as O Toyo. When he took the air with her he noticed a large, fine-looking cat following them and watching them closely but he thought nothing of it. One night the beautiful O Toyo woke suddenly to find the cat upon her bed and before she could scream the cat had throttled her. The cat scratched a grave, buried her body and assumed the favorite lady's form. When dawn came all believed that it was O Toyo who lay sleeping in her bed.

The prince himself did not notice any change so perfect was the transformation and so closely had the cat observed their ways together, but gradually he found himself growing weaker and weaker, for whilst he slept the cat was draining him of his life blood. One of the prince's servants, who understood these things, guessed what might have happened and trapped the evil creature by a stratagen forcing it to turn back into a cat. But with a cat's agility she escaped and took refuge in the mountains where later the prince arranged a spectacular hunt which tracked it down and ended its wicked life.

In the paradoxical way that symbolism and the supernatural can operate in two quite contradictory directions at the same time, the cat for whom so much ill was felt could also bring good luck. Even as recently as 1929 a newspaper report suggested that York County in Pennsylvania was almost stripped of black cats because a local fear of witchcraft had led people to employ a charm against the devil which involved plunging a live black cat into boiling water and keeping one of its bones as an amulet. There are regional contradictions: the black cat which an American considers unlucky will, despite its supposed connexion with the devil, bring good luck to an Englishman.

One strange practice, which persisted into the present century, was the burial of cats in the walls or foundations of buildings as a magical charm to bring luck, to keep the house vermin free or as a building sacrifice. Many instances have been discovered where the animal could

The true portraiture of RICHARD WHITINGTON thrise Lord Maior of London a vertuous and godly man full off good Works (and those famous) he builded the Gate of London called Newgate which before was a miserable doungeon. He builded Whitington Colledge & made it an Almose house for poore people Also he builded a greate parte of y hospitall of S. Bartholomewes in westsmithfield in London. He also builded the beautifull Library at y Gray Friers in Londõ, called Christes Hospitall; Also he builded the Guilde Halle Chappell and increased a greate parte of the East ende of the saied halle, beside many other good workes.

R. Elstrack sculpsit.

The engraving **(left)** of Lord Mayor Richard Whittington is not so accurate as it claims. In the painting on which it was based his hand originally rested on a skull, not a cat. Dick's cat may have been a boat.

not have been accidentally walled up. The pose of the body does not suggest accidental entombment, with the consequent panic and strain of death, and sometimes appears to be consciously arranged in a hunting posture to terrify the rats. Human sacrifices used to be made to ensure a building's safety and present-day burial of coins and other objects is a survival of this propitiatory magic.

In the south of France there was wide belief in magician cats, called *matagots,* who could bring prosperity to a house where they were loved and well cared for. Buddhist tradition says that a light-colored cat will always ensure silver in the house and that the home with a dark-colored cat will never lack gold.

Most famous of *matagots* is perhaps that of Dick Whittington, four times Lord Mayor of London, who according to the folk tale, though not history, owed all his fortune to it. Young Dick was a poor boy from Gloucestershire who walked in search of fame and fortune to London, where the streets, he had been told, were 'paved with gold'. Arriving in the city and discovering that the tales were not, at least not literally, true he found a scullion's job with the wealthy merchant Fitzwarren. With his first wages he bought a cat to keep down the rats in his tiny attic. When the other servants all invested in a trading voyage of their master's Dick ventured all he had—the cat. Despairing of success he started to walk back to his village, but on Highgate Hill, overlooking London, the bells of the city seemed to call him to 'Turn again, Whittington.' Hopeful, he went back to his garret.

When the ship arrived at a spice island of the Orient the palace of the king was found to be overrun with rats. Puss soon vanquished them, earning the king's gratitude in the shape of a princely fortune for her owner, who was thus set on his way to become one of the greatest merchants of medieval London.

Although there is a portrait in London's Guildhall showing Lord Mayor Whittington with a cat, it dates from long after his death in 1423 and the legend has been variously explained by saying the cat was a catboat—a one-masted vessel used for coal and timber—which made him a fortune in the trade in coal from Newcastle to London, or an *achat* (purchase).

Whether Whittington had a cat or not the story follows a pattern current in the folklore of Denmark, Persia and Italy a hundred years before Whittington. One of the best known versions was told by Charles Perrault in his fairy tale of Puss-in-Boots—the poor boy's cat which tricks a king into believing that his master is a rich and powerful landowner, acquires him wealth by outwitting and killing a wicked ogre, and wins him a princess as a bride.

The 'Harmless, Necessary' Cat

Ballerina Anna Pavlova with her cat. Unless frightened, most cats are very gentle and will not dig their claws into bare skin.

It would be wrong to think of the history of the cat as being largely a matter of religion and magic—black or white. Most of the time it has been to man what it is today, rodent catcher and domestic friend.

The cat has been loved and respected throughout the Moslem world, not as a religious symbol, but because Mohammed himself is said to have loved cats. On one occasion his favorite cat fell asleep in the sleeve of his gown and rather than disturb the pet he cut off the sleeve. Another story tells how a snake crawled into his sleeve for warmth and when asked to leave, refused. The prophet suggested that the matter be referred to the cat and the snake consented. The cat asked the snake to put his head out of the sleeve to discuss the situation and the snake complied, whereupon the cat seized hold of it, pulled it from the sleeve and carried it away.

A first-century Irish god was said to be cat-headed; cats also play a magical part in some early Celtic legends, but they were appreciated more for their practical value. In an old Welsh law it was decreed that if a marriage was dissolved the household goods were divided but the husband took the cat. Any cats over the first went to the wife.

Kittens were thought of as children's playthings, but adult cats were listed as one of those necessary items of daily life which might be the legal property of a woman. The value and tiethi (qualities) of a cat were outlined in the laws promulgated by the Welsh king Hywel the Good, who died in AD 948. Later the value was increased and the requirements made more detailed: the cat had to be 'perfect of ear, perfect of eye, perfect of teeth, perfect of claw, and *without marks of fire*.' Presumably these were not brands but scorch marks which would indicate a lazy cat who sat too long by the fire and perhaps give mice and rats and extra warning of its presence by the smell of singed fur. In this later law cats were valued according to their owner. Hywel's laws appear to apply only to the female. Were males not considered good mousers? What was a good tom worth? Not only Welsh law put high value on the cat; Henry the Fowler, ninth-century king of Saxony, decreed that anyone who killed an adult cat should be fined sixty bushels of corn.

Despite the disapproval of the early Christian Church the cat was not always treated as the agent of the devil and many churchmen can be numbered among its friends. A much loved cat was the only companion of the great sixth-century Pope Gregory I when he put aside the papal tiara to return to simple monastic life. An Irish monk wrote a delightful poem about his cat "Pangur Ban" which Robin Flower translated into modern English, of which this is one verse:

I and Pangur Ban, my cat,
'Tis a like task we are at;
Hunting mice is his delight,
Hunting words I sit all night.

A cat was the only animal allowed to the female hermits under the strict discipline of the Cistercian order. 'Ye mine leove sustren,' says the *Ancren Riwle* (Anchoress's Rule), 'ne schulen haben no Best bute Kat one.' (You, my beloved sisters, shall have no beast but one cat.) The monkish writers who compiled the early bestiaries and natural histories of the Middle Ages observed their mousers carefully; the English monk Bartholomew, writing about 1260, noted how the cat 'is led by a straw and playeth therewith and is a right heavy beste in age, and full slepy and lieth slyly in wait for mice.' While most of their contemporaries thought of the cat only as a rodent catcher the monks in their meditative life had time to see the cat as companion and friend, though not always a well-behaved one.

John Skelton (1460–1529) in his long poem 'Philip Sparrow' laments the death of the pet bird of one of the Black Nuns of Carrow in the north of England:

From me was taken away
By Gib, our cat savage
That in furious rage
Caught Phillip by the head,
And slew him there starke dead.

If it is frightened a cat bristles all over making its fur stand on end and its tail bush out so that it will seem a more formidable opponent. The kitten **(left)** has already got the idea.

Pope Gregory I was not the only prince of the church to care for cats. A similar story is told of Pope Gregory III, and Leo XII had a cat called Micetto which, shortly before his death, he presented to the French statesman the Vicomte de Chateaubriand, who wrote of it when it had grown into a 'big greyish-red cat with black stripes across it.' 'It was born in the Vatican, in the Loggia of Raphael. Pope Leo XII brought it up in a fold of his robes where I often used to look at it with envy when the Pope gave me an audience. It was known as "the Pope's cat" and as such used to enjoy the special attentions of pious ladies. I am trying to make it forget its exile, the Sistine Chapel, the sun on Michelangelo's cupola, where it used to walk far above the earth. . . .'

Thomas Wolsey, Cardinal and Chancellor to Henry VIII of England, also had a cat which accompanied him to religious services and diplomatic audiences. Wolsey cared for it so highly that the Venetian ambassador compared the pair to Caligula and his horse. Richelieu, another powerful statesman-cardinal, introduced a whole colony of cats to the court of France. He had them brought to play with him before he rose each day and on his death left provision for his fourteen surviving cats to be well cared for. Unfortunately the cats suffered for his unpopularity and instead of living in the luxury arranged for them, were killed by Swiss mercenaries. Richelieu's contemporary William Laud, Archbishop of Canterbury, was another great cat fancier—though perhaps a less fortunate one!

France's Louis XV had a white cat which used to come to his bedroom every morning. Louis' interest in cats was due to the enthusiasm of his queen, Marie Leczinska, who was passionately attached to them. On one occasion the king surprised the Duc de Noailles, who was terrified of cats, by creeping up behind him, grasping his neck and giving a loud and savage miaow. The poor duke fainted right away and was so difficult to rouse that it was feared he had breathed his last.

Politicians and heads of state in more democratic times have given the cat homes in high places. Abraham Lincoln found three half frozen cats on a visit to General Grant's camp during the Civil War, and adopted them. Theodore Roosevelt's cat Slippers attended White House dinners and state occasions. Winston Churchill had a ginger tom who would join him when he presided at wartime cabinet meetings. Harold Wilson, also an occupant of 10 Downing Street, took with him Nemo, the family Siamese. The French Premier Léon Blum also had a Siamese, as did Raymond Poincaré. Georges Clémenceau had a Blue Persian specially brought over from Britain to live with him in the Elysée Palace. The Italian fascist Mussolini and the Russian revolutionary leader Lenin both loved cats, however different their views about their fellow men.

All the incidents depicted in Pieter Brueghel the Elder's *Netherland Proverbs* (**above**) illustrate proverbs popularly known in the middle ages. The soldier in armour leaning on the wall demonstrates his version of the story of Belling the Cat.

All cats and kittens need somewhere to stretch and exercise their claws. Provide a proper scratching place and they will not damage your furnishings.

If you forget your cat's mealtime you may find that it has helped itself. Your cat — and Siamese in particular — will expect more than food from you. They will appreciate it if you set aside a little time each day to play with them.

There is no evidence that cats played any part in the Russian Revolution. Six centuries earlier, however, the English poet William Langland used a cat to represent the cruel nobility in a poem that played its part in the launching of an early attempt at a popular uprising: the Peasants' Revolt. In the prologue to his *Vision of Piers the Plowman* Langland takes the popular medieval fable of the belling of the cat and uses it to represent the political state of the time. A council of rats and mice, representing the English Commons, meet to discuss their safety and in particular what to do about a great cat (probably representing John of Gaunt) who plays with them as he chooses. If they protest they fear reprisals. One elegant rat, who has seen the rich men of London with chains about their necks, going everywhere and causing trouble, suggests that if they had bells on their chains men could hear them coming 'and awey renne'. Similarly if they could hang a bell around the neck of the cat they could get out of the way. The council agreed and a bell was bought and hung upon a collar but no one dared attach it to the cat.

Langland's contemporary, Geoffrey Chaucer, alludes to the cat in several of his Canterbury Tales. There is a well-known passage in *The Manciple's Tale*:

Lat take a cat and fostre him wel with milk
And tendre flessch and make his couche of silk,
And let him seen a mouse go by the wal,
Anon he weyvith milk and flessch and al,
And every deyntee that is in that hous,
Suich appetit he hath to ete a mous.

William Shakespeare's friend the Earl of Southampton was painted with his favourite cat who climbed down a chimney to join his master when he was imprisoned in the Tower of London.

There have been many writers, painters and musicians who have admired the cat, though in literature it has not always held an honored position. In Aesop's fables, for instance, cats are usually the enemy; and in the popular medieval romance of Reynard the Fox the cat Sir Tybert, though treated badly, is not given much sympathy. Even in Puss-in-Boots it is the cat's cunning and deceit which is the key to the story. Outside fable it has not been often that the cat has been at the center of a story but in *Gammer Gurton's Needle*, first performed in 1548, 'Gyb our cat' starts the whole plot in motion by trying to steal some milk, thereby distracting Grandma who loses her precious needle. Later her serving-man Hodge mistakes the cat's eyes for glowing embers in the hearth. Gyb is wrongly accused of stealing some bacon, and almost slaughtered in case she has swallowed the needle, but eventually it is found embedded in Hodge's behind and all ends happily.

Shakespeare does not have much to say about the cat, and his kindest remark is to describe it as 'harmless, necessary', but his friend and patron Henry Wriothesley, the young Earl of Southampton, was painted with a solemn black and white cat as companion when he was imprisoned in the Tower of London for his part in the rebellion of the Earl of Essex against Elizabeth I. A century later the antiquarian Thomas Pennant claimed, though we have no proof of the story, that it was his favorite cat which had found its way to the Tower, forced an entrance and reached its master by climbing down the chimney of his lodging.

Ill-fated Mary, Queen of Scots, during her long imprisonment, embroidered a set of wall hangings, one panel of which is clearly labelled "A Catte". It shows a prick-eared tabby sitting beside a rat or mouse. It has been suggested that Mary meant the cat to represent Elizabeth I, who kept her prisoner, and the mouse was herself.

Portraits of cats were extremely unusual until much later times, though Wenceslaus Hollar engraved a famous portrait (if not a very attractive one) of the cat of the Grand Duke of Muscovy. However, they are often part of the picture. Leonardo da Vinci did some delightful sketches of cats: for example an infant Jesus holds one in a *Virgin and Child*. Rembrandt has

"A Catte" embroidered by Mary Queen of Scots. In the right-hand arm of the cross is a plump mouse. Did the unfortunate queen think of herself as the mouse and Elizabeth I of England as the cat?

In this engraving from William Hogarth's *Scenes of Cruelty* he has shown two cats strung up from a post and another with two balloons attached being flung from an attic window.

a cat in a small etching of the Holy Family and Giacomo da Barroccio painted a Holy Family with a cat looking up at a bird held high by the infant John the Baptist. Dürer places a cat at the foot of the Tree of Knowledge in an engraving of Adam and Eve. Tintoretto includes evil-looking cats in paintings of the *Annunciation* and the *Last Supper*. Ghirlandaio painted a *Last Supper* with a cat sitting next to Judas to symbolize the devil. Hieronymus Bosch puts a cat in his *Garden of Delights,* and a frightened cat is being chased in his *Adoration of the Magi*. The Elder Brueghel includes cats in his *Death of the Virgin, Procession to Calvary* and an illustration of the fable of the Belling of the Cat in his *Netherland Proverbs*. His son Jan painted an inquisitive cat peering out of a loft above the stable in his *Adoration of the Magi*. They were precursors of the Dutch and Flemish genre painters of later years who quite naturally depicted cats in their quiet domestic scenes.

Before the witchcraft hysteria swept Europe and put the cat in deep disfavor one of its greatest friends was the French essayist and philosopher Michel Eyquem de Montaigne who allowed his cat to accompany him to the tower he built as a retreat from the folly and wickedness of the world. He compared his companion with himself: 'When my cat and I entertain each other with mutual apish tricks, as playing with a garter, who knows but I make my cat more sport than she makes me?'

The periods of persecution of the cat did not save man from evil but put him into greater danger, for the cat was the only means of controlling the rapidly growing rat population which from time to time was responsible for the spread of plague and pestilence. Unfortunately no one realised the role played by the rat and, in London in 1665 for instance, the regulations against the movement of domestic animals led to the destruction of many cats, who were themselves thought to be carriers of plague.

With the eighteenth century the cat began to come into its own. As today, it had its persecutors—Hogarth's *Scenes of Cruelty* shows two cats strung from a post and another being thrown out of a window attached to a pair of inflated balloons—but its admirers began to increase if the evidence of art and literature is to be believed. John Gay, the English poet and dramatist

48

who wrote *The Beggar's Opera*, included the cat in two of his fables in verse. One sets up a lazy cat against a human rat catcher, in the other an old woman blames her cats for people calling her a witch. The cats reply:

> *Had we ne'er starved beneath your roof,*
> *We had, like others of our race,*
> *In credit liv'd, as beasts of chase.*
> *'Tis infamy to serve a hag;*
> *Cats are thought imps, her brooms a nag;*
> *And boys against our lives combine,*
> *Because, 'tis said, your cats have nine.*

John Rich, the actor who presented and played in *The Beggar's Opera* (thereby it was said making Gay rich and Rich gay), was a cat fanatic. One famous actress, visiting him for the first time, found him surrounded by no less than twenty-seven cats—on his lap, on his shoulders, drinking the cream for his tea and even sitting on his head!

A few years later, when Samuel Johnson compiled his famous *Dictionary* he defined the cat as 'a domestic animal that catches mice, commonly reckoned by naturalists the lowest order of the leonine species'. The description gives little idea of the affection in which the good doctor held his own pets. His biographer and amanuensis, James Boswell, could not abide cats —he was probably allergic to them—but where the doctor was there were cats. As Boswell wrote in his famous *Life of Samuel Johnson*:

I shall never forget the indulgence with which he treated Hodge, his cat; for whom he himself used to go out and buy oysters, lest the servants having that trouble should take a dislike to the poor creature. I am, unluckily, one of those who have an antipathy to a cat, so that I am uneasy when in the room with one; and I own, I frequently suffered a good deal from the presence of the same Hodge. I recollect him one day scrambling up Dr. Johnson's breast, apparently with much satisfaction, while my friend, smiling and half-whistling, rubbed down his back, and pulled him by the tail; and when I observed he was a fine cat, saying, 'Why, yes, Sir, but I have had cats whom I liked better than this,' and then, as if perceiving Hodge to be out of countenance, adding, 'but he is a very fine cat, a very fine cat indeed.'

Dr. Johnson befriended the poet and scholar Christopher Smart who developed a religious mania and was eventually confined in the asylum of Bedlam. In the madhouse his companion was his cat Jeoffry and in an inspired if somewhat obscure poem which he called *Jubilate Agno* (*Rejoice in the Lamb*) he devotes a long and beautiful section to 'considering his cat Jeoffry' (see page 8).

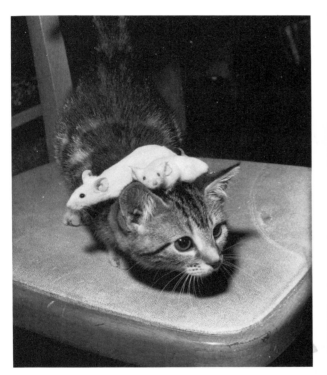

Opposite: Peg Woffington visits John Rich in his home, where she found him surrounded by his twenty-seven cats.

Studies of cats from the sketch book of Jean
Antoine Watteau (1684-1721).

The three Misses Walpole, painted by
George James in 1768.

William Cowper, another eighteenth-century poet, author of the famous *John Gilpin*, recorded his cats in verses based on actual incidents. *The Colubriad*, constructed in epic form, tells of a cat's encounter with a snake, and *The Retired Cat* recounts how the poet's cat 'sedate and grave' made herself comfortable in a half-open linen drawer and was accidentally shut in for two whole days. Perhaps it was this cat in younger days whom Cowper described in a letter to a cousin:

I have a kitten, my dear, the drollest of all creatures that ever wore a cat's skin. Her gambols are not to be described and would be incredible if they could. In point of size she is likely to be a kitten always, being extremely small of her age, but time, I suppose, that spoils everything, will make her a cat. You will see her, I hope, before that melancholy period shall arrive, for no wisdom that she may gain by experience and reflection hereafter will compensate the loss of her present hilarity. She is dressed in a tortoise-shell suit and I know that you will delight in her.

Not only writers began to take an interest in cats. They appear in the rustic studies and animal pictures of English painters such as Francis Barlow and George Morland. When George Stubbs painted his portrait of the racehorse Arabian Godolphin the horse was restless without the company of a particular cat friend and so the cat was included in the picture too. When the horse died the cat refused to leave its body until it was taken away for burial, and then disappeared. Her body was found later in a hayloft.

In France, in particular, where the court made cats fashionable, François Desportes included cats in his still lifes of game and Jean Baptiste Oudry made some enchanting studies. Court painters like Watteau, Boucher and Fragonard all put cats into their pictures. Watteau made a careful study of the animal but, despite their skill, his successors rarely produced anything more than a smudge of fur. Much more alive are the cats which appear in Jean Baptiste Chardin's homely interiors or in portraits like Jean Baptiste Perronneau's *Girl with a Kitten*.

The Swiss painter Gottfried Mind was passionately fond of cats; the only animals he painted were cats and bears. It is told that when he was an apprentice he criticized his master's rendering of a cat and was challenged to do better. After that he always painted the cats in his teacher's pictures.

'Stately, Kindly, Lordly' Friend

Left: Sir Walter Scott with Hinse.
Above: A Russian woodcut.

During the nineteenth century the cat strengthened its place in man's affections and attracted many devoted admirers. Sometimes the relationship was awash with sentimentality though not in John Keats' poem *On Mrs. Reynolds' Cat* which is understandingly addressed to an ageing pet. Nor could one accuse the French painter Théodore Géricault of being sentimental. He is said to have had his models shaved so that he could see the anatomy beneath the fur. It was Géricault's paintings that encouraged other artists to present the cat as a gentle and loving pet instead of in its frequent role of thief and scavenger. Millet, Courbet, Manet, Renoir, Gauguin, Bonnard—all painted cats, but the most famous cat artist in France was, in fact, a Swiss: Théophile Alexandre Steinlen. Steinlen's cats were not the pampered pets of the fashionable salons but the cats of the rooftops and the gutters of Paris.

Sir Edwin Landseer, who carved the lions in London's Trafalgar Square, painted some very realistic pictures of cats when he was a young man but apparently was not satisfied with them and never painted cats later, though he painted many of dogs. Novelist Sir Walter Scott was also more loyal to dogs, except for a cat called Hinse of Hinsfeldt which was his constant companion but sat at a distance replacing the dog at his master's side only when it went out.

A later artist with the same popular appeal as Landseer was Louis Wain who, towards the end of the century, launched a flood of cat pictures upon the English public. Unlike Steinlen he often dressed his cats in human clothes and produced drawings that were really caricature, but as a cat-lover, a breeder and a show judge, he knew cats well, and claimed he drew them as he saw them. When his pictures are free of jokiness and cloying sentimentality they can be very good indeed. Wain became a schizophrenic and in his pictures of that period the cat becomes more and more part of a decorative background, often beautiful but profoundly disturbing.

All kinds of interpretations have been put upon the fantasies of Lewis Carroll, the creator of *Alice's Adventures in Wonderland* and *Through the Looking Glass,* but whatever the learned mathematician may have been hiding in his stories, Alice's cat Dinah at least starts off as a 'dear, quiet thing : . . purring so nicely by the fire, licking her paws and washing her face'. Certainly at the end of *Through the Looking Glass* neither Dinah nor her kittens will be drawn into discussion about their role in the story:

' "Now, Kitty, let's consider who it was that dreamed it all. This is a serious question, my dear, and you should *not* go on licking your paw like that—as if Dinah hadn't washed you this morning! You see, Kitty, it *must* have been either me or the Red King. . . . You were his wife, my dear, so you ought to know—oh Kitty, *do* help to settle it! I'm sure your paw can wait!" But the provoking kitten began on the other paw, and pretended it hadn't heard the question.'

The title page of Theophile Steinlen's book of 'designs without words' and one of them: *The Ball of Thread.*

John Tenniel's original illustration for the Cheshire Cat in chapter six of *Alice in Wonderland.*

In *Wonderland* the Cheshire Cat has much more to say for himself: why he is mad, for instance:

' "To begin with," said the Cat, "a dog's not mad. You grant that?"

' "I suppose so," said Alice.

' "Well, then," the cat went on, "you see a dog growls when it's angry, and wags its tail when it's pleased. Now *I* growl when I'm pleased and wag my tail when I'm angry. Therefore I'm mad." '

Edward Lear was another great nonsense writer and involves cats in many of his verses. *The Owl and the Pussy Cat*, the Runcible Cat with its crimson whiskers, and the cats who chase a Clangle Wangle, have found admirers in every generation since they were created. But the most important cat in Lear's life went by the name of Foss. For seventeen years Foss was his companion and he left some amusing sketches of him.

Algernon Swinburne, William Wordsworth and Alfred Tennyson all wrote poems about cats. For example, Tennyson's *The Spinster's Sweet-Arts* is in Lincolnshire dialect and tells of a spinster who named her four cats after the wooers she had rejected who would

niver 'a cotch'd ony mice, but 'a left me the work to do,
And ta'en to the bottle beside, so es all that I 'ears be true;

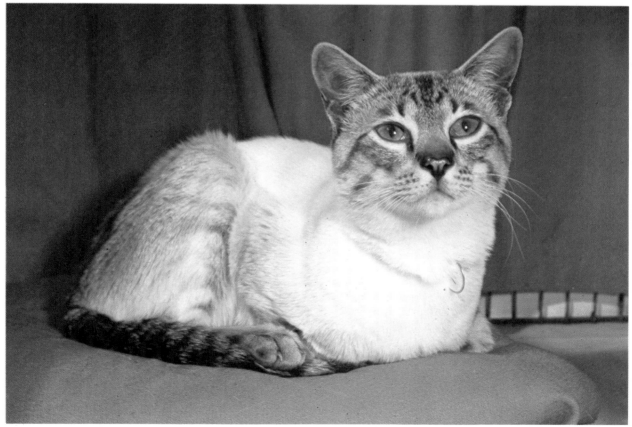

William Makepeace Thackeray, who wrote *Vanity Fair*, must have liked cats. Thackeray's daughters used to look after a whole family of strays which they named after characters in Dickens' novels, and Thackeray's favorite, Louisa, was allowed to eat from his own plate at breakfast. Charles Dickens himself does not paint a very friendly picture of cats in his many books but this does not mean that he did not like them. His daughter Mary described one evening in her book *My Father as I Recall Him*:

We were all, except father, going to a ball, and when we started, we left "the master" and his cat in the drawing-room together. "The Master" was reading at a small table; suddenly the candle went out. My father, who was much interested in his book, relighted the candle, stroked the cat, who was looking at him pathetically he noticed, and continued his reading. A few minutes later, as the light became dim, he looked up just in time to see puss deliberately put out the candle with his paw, and then look appealing at him. This second and unmistakable hint was not disregarded and puss was given the petting he craved.

Of other nineteenth-century literary giants Théophile Gautier wrote of his own cats in *La Ménagerie Intime*; Honoré de Balzac, Victor Hugo and Emile Zola often introduced them into their novels and Balzac even wrote a satire on English society *Peines de Coeur d'une Chatte*

Tom and Jerry **(above left)** in the popular cartoon-film series. But why does the cat always get the **worst of things?**
Jean Cocteau **(above right)** with painter Foujita and the cat on which he based the make-up for the beast in his film of *Beauty and the Beast*.

Anglaise (*Love Life of an English Cat*). Hippolyte Taine wrote twelve sonnets and Charles Baudelaire three magnificent poems to the cat. Madame de Staël, who hated cats until she was imprisoned in a cell that ran with rats and was given a cat to keep them down, became their great admirer. The painter Jean Auguste Ingres was devoted to his cat Patrocle. Madame Récamier, Prosper Mérimée, Guy de Maupassant, the critic Charles Sainte-Beuve—France seemed to challenge the world in the number of its cat-lovers as though to make up for Napoleon Bonaparte's dislike and fear of them.

That fine Englishwoman Florence Nightingale, whose work during the Crimean War and after laid the foundations of modern nursing, paid her homage to the cat:

I learned the lesson of life from a little kitten of mine, one of two. The old cat comes in and says, very cross, 'I didn't ask you in here. I like to have my Missis to myself.' The bigger and handsomer kitten runs away; but the little one stands her ground: *and when the old enemy comes near enough kisses his nose and makes the peace. That is the lesson of life; to kiss one's enemy's nose always standing one's ground.*

In America it was Mark Twain toward the end of the nineteenth century who made the definitive statement that: 'A home without a cat, and a well-fed, well-petted and properly revered cat, may be a perfect home, *perhaps*, but how can it prove its title?'

As one moves into the twentieth century the rollcall of the cats' friends becomes even longer, Pierre Loti, Anatole France, Colette and Jean Cocteau; all loved and wrote about their cats. T. S. Eliot wrote a whole collection of poems in *Old Possum's Book of Practical Cats* which, though light-hearted nonsense, reveal a real understanding of cat behavior. Doris Lessing's book *Particularly Cats* contains some of the most perceptive studies of the human-cat relationship. Tennessee Williams tells the strange story of Nitchevo in *The Malediction* and Truman Capote gives Cat an important role in *Breakfast at Tiffany's*, while in the stories of *archie and mehitabel* Don Marquis invented the definitive independent alley cat.

One could go on to enumerate the musical cats, like the cat in Scarlatti's *Cat's Fugue*, or the Siamese in Ravel's *L'Enfant et les Sortilèges*; balletic cats, in *The Sleeping Beauty, Les Demoiselles de Nuit*; film cats, from Pinocchio's *Figaro* to Tom of *Tom and Jerry,* and performing cats like Rhubard or Pywacket in *Bell, Book and Candle* . . . but that would take a library of books.

Cats of the East

The cat was known in China as early as 2000 BC, but there is no evidence that it was domesticated there until many centuries later. Both China and Japan call the cat Mau—the same word as in ancient Egypt—and this has been held to be proof that Egypt was their origin. It is certainly evidence that all cats speak the same language, but no more. It is possible that Egyptian cats gradually spread across the whole of Asia. They were known in Persia by the sixth century AD, for there was already a word for the domestic cat in the language of Zend which was replaced by Persian about this time, and there are pictures of cats in Persian manuscripts. By this time also they were already known in India where the legendary cat Patripatan climbed up to heaven.

The Hindu word for cat means 'the cleanest' and they became protected by Orthodox Hindu rites.

According to legend, Confucius, who lived in the fifth century BC, had a favorite cat, but the evidence suggests that they were domesticated in China only about AD 400. In some places, as in Europe, the cat became involved in fertility rites, but they were valued largely as destroyers of rats and mice. They were particularly used to protect silkworms from rats and, despite occasional tales of wicked cats, acquired the reputation of being able to keep evil away. If no real cat was available a picture painted on the wall sufficed.

At one time it was believed that a special breed of cat with drooping ears existed in China. Several eighteenth and nineteenth-century naturalists recorded the fact and in 1896 a seaman actually brought one back claiming it was one of a type bred to be eaten. Not until 1938 was another located, which proved to be a rare mutation. Perhaps the earlier reports were actually of Chinese lion dogs (Pekinese) which in many Chinese paintings look very like cats.

Cats probably reached Japan at the same time as Buddhism, in the sixth century, though

The apparition of a giant cat—an incident from a Japanese legend, in a print by the cat-loving artist Atagawa Kuniyoshi (1798-1861).

according to legend they did not arrive until four centuries later when the Emperor Ichi-Jo imported a white cat from China which presented him with five pure white kittens at the imperial palace of Kyoto. So delighted was the Emperor that he decreed that they should be brought up with as much care as children of the imperial family. In Japan the cat became a pampered pet, kept on a lead, and painted and pottery cats were used to protect the crops and the silkworms from the ravages of rodent pests. Unfortunately they failed to do the job and the cat's prestige began to fall. Stories of evil cats began to be told and, as in Europe, they were linked with witches. At last in AD 1602 a law was passed that all adult cats should be set free; trading in cats and even giving them as presents was forbidden.

Soon cats were restored to a more natural place in the scale of things, but Japanese legend is full of tales of cats—witches' cats with forked tails, metamorphosed cats, even vampire cats (see page 60). Every temple had its cat to guard its manuscripts from mice and one cat, Maneki-Neko, waylaid so many passers-by and lured them to her lowly temple that she became a famous cat and her temple a wealthy one. Now it has become a shrine with a cemetery for cats where Tokyo cat-lovers bring offerings and small cat figures to help their pets to heaven. On the temple facade row upon row of cats are painted with raised paws to represent Maneki-Neko's gestures of greeting which has also become a symbol of good luck. Good luck also comes with a tortoiseshell cat and Japanese sailors in particular like to have a tortoiseshell aboard ship. It used to be believed that they could foretell approaching storms and if sent to the top of the mast could frighten the storm demons away.

Such is the Japanese affinity for cats that her artists have managed to capture the myriad moods of their pets in a way unchallenged by any European painter. Outstanding among them are Utamaro (died 1806) and Kuniyoshi (1769–1861) whose prints, whether of domestic cats or legendary ones, are unequaled.

Breeds

For centuries the development of different kinds of cat was a matter of natural selection, occasional mutation and cross-breeding with closely related species. The domestic cat of Egypt was already a species clearly differentiated from the local and European wildcat. A similar development presumably took place in other parts of the world so that house cats bred with house cats more frequently than with wildcats and clear strains began to develop. Of course, human beings with a preference for a particular cat's appearance or character must have played their part in trying to control mating.

Different kinds of cats developed in different parts of the world but the names certain breeds have today should not be taken as an indication of the area where they first appeared. Paintings and descriptions survive which give us occasional glimpses of what particular cats were like. The Egyptian house cat, like the European wildcat, had tabby markings and a tabby pattern breaks through in many breeds and certainly in those breeds of European origin. The great cat authority, R. I. Pocock (1863–1947), suggested regional developments: red from the Cape of Good Hope, a reddish-yellow with a sharp nose from Central America, a short-tailed black and white from Japan, a black cat from the south of Russia, a blackish coloring from Southern Africa, a bluish-gray from Europe and Siberia, a fawn and black from Siam and a tortoisehell traditionally said to come from Spain.

Surprisingly, the most common domestic cat of Britain was not the tabby, if we are to believe the antiquarian John Aubrey who, writing some years later about Archbishop Laud, 'a great lover of Catts', describes how he 'was presented with some Cyprus-catts, i.e. our Tabby-catts, which were sold, at first for 5 pounds a piece: this was about 1637, or 1638. I do well remember that the common English Catt, was white with some blewish piedness: sc. a gallipot blew. The race or breed of them are now almost lost.' Gallipot was a kind of turpentine. Aubrey was a great gossip and not the most reliable of sources. Was this blue and white cat the kind which the Virginian colonists took to the New World or which came to America on the *Mayflower* (for tabbies are still called 'Cyprus Cats' in East Anglia where many of the Pilgrims had their homes), or did the Pilgrim Fathers take a cat from Leyden, perhaps a tabby like the one shown in an early seventeenth-century Dutch interior drawn by Johannes Stradamus? Edward Topsell in his *The Historie of Four-Fottes Beastes*, published thirteen years before the Pilgrim Fathers set foot on American soil, said 'Cats are of divers colours, but for the most part griseld, like to congealed ise.'

It was not until the nineteenth century that people began to take a serious interest in the breeding of cats, encouraged by the introduction of foreign types. The first cat show was held at the Crystal Palace in London in 1871 and became an annual event. The first British Cat Club was founded in 1887. The first cat show in the United States of which there are records was part of a large livestock and pet show held in 1884 and the first separate cat show was in 1895, organised by an Englishman called Hyde, who had visited one of the Crystal Palace shows. The first cat club in the United States was the Beresford Cat Club of Chicago, founded in 1899.

Most cats are born from random matings which they choose themselves, but controled breeding has now produced new strains as well as developing the characteristics of existing cat types. With the establishment of cat clubs and breed societies, agreement was reached on exact characteristics for different types of cat—though from club to club these may differ slightly. In Britain the Governing Council of the Cat Fancy, which was formed from the National Cat Club in 1910, lays down the rules for the whole country but there is no single authority for the whole of the United States.

To begin with, breeders presumably simply tried to reproduce the characteristics of an existing type without variation, then they began to cross-breed to achieve new variations or selectively breed mutations to emphasise a particular characteristic. There is often criticism in the cat world that some breeders are distorting the original beauty of the cat and that inbreeding is damaging the personality of the cat. The main role of the breeder is to preserve the existing breed but new breeds are occasionally acknowledged. To establish a new breed the cats must obviously have characteristics which are different or in different combination from existing breeds and these characteristics must be transmitted hereditarily. It is not necessary for them to show in all direct descendants, but they must recur in sufficient matings and in subsequent generations for the characteristics to be considered 'fixed'. A pedigree cat is one whose antecedants are known for several generations and who breed true, that is to say that all the kittens resemble the parents.

Genetic research has shown that certain characteristics are dominant over others and some recessive. Silver, for instance, is recessive to a full colored coat, brown is a recessive color, Burmese is dominant over Siamese and the gene which gives more than the usual number of toes is dominant. There are two apparently paired conditions which are improperly understood and which breeders have not yet mastered. Tortoiseshell males, if they survive, are always sterile and white cats with blue eyes are frequently deaf.

The descriptions of breeds which follow are intended to give the general reader a clear idea of each of the main breeds, but since requirements differ slightly from club to club, it is important that owners intending to show their cats in competition should ascertain the requirements of the club in organising the show.

Body Shape

There are three basic body types. The occidental cat has a thick body, short legs and strong bones, with a rounded face, short snout, rounded eyes and shortish ears. Oriental cats, usually grouped as 'foreign', have much lighter bones, long bodies and long legs. They lack the chubby cheeks of the occidental cat and their heads have a pointed look, emphasised by their sloping eyes and tall, pointed ears. Thirdly, there is the Manx, the tailless cat, whose longer rear legs elevate its rump and give it a hoppity, rabbit-like gait.

Coat

There are two basic kinds of coat, long-hair and short-hair, but intermediate lengths often occur. Breeders try to achieve clearly long and short hair only and to avoid wooliness. The Rex cat, a relatively recent and artificially created breed, has curly hair.

Color

Cats have a wide range of coat color. Brown, gray, white, silver, black and cream are all self-explanatory, but the cat world also uses blue (to mean gray with a bluish tinge), red (which means ginger, marmalade or even orange or a yellowish color) and lilac (gray with a mauvish tinge). The color of visible skin (known as leather) on the nose and paws may be black, pink, gray or 'red'. Eyes are most frequently green but may be blue, shades of brown through to orange and yellow, or black. In some breeds it is quite acceptable for one of a cat's eyes to be of a different color from the other.

Long-haired Breeds

All long-haired cats should have silky, long flowing coats without any trace of wooliness. They have a ruff of long hair around the neck like that of the lion and the shortish tail is full to its tip. The body should be low and cobby, that is thickset on short legs. The head should be wide and round with a short broad nose. The ears, smallish and set at the side of the head, are tufted and round-tipped. The eyes are large and round. Long-haired cats used to be called Persian cats or Angoras. In fact there were two distinct breeds but cross-breeding was common in the early years of this century and the Persian characteristics proved dominant. Some people consider the feral coon cats of Maine and Massachusetts to be Angoras. They are certainly long-haired cats which went wild. Angoras were introduced to Italy about 1550 and to France at the end of the sixteenth century. They were believed to come from Ankara in Turkey and that is how they got their name. In fact the Angora had a wedge-shaped head rather than a round one, medium-sized ears and slightly sloping eyes. Their fur was silkier than that of the Persians. The present shape is largely the result of breeding and also partly perhaps a change of diet and climate. Both types reached America either through Europe or were introduced by traders from the Orient during the eighteenth century.

There is a type of cat still known in Turkey as the Ankara cat whose coat is all white and which has one green eye and one blue.

Long-haired White

The coat of this breed should be pure white without a single colored hair. The eyes may be either deep blue or orange and some clubs consider an odd-eyed cat with one blue and one orange eye to be acceptable. However blue-eyed cats in which an area of orange appears in one or both eyes, or vice versa, are not acceptable. In Britain two separate breeds are recognised according to eye color. The blue-eyed type is the original breed. The orange-eyed cat is the result of mating with Blue, Black or Cream Long-Haired females. Blue-eyed whites are frequently deaf and rarely have good hearing. Odd-eyed cats are consequently often used for breeding. White cats do not necessarily come from two white parents. A mating with a Long-Haired Black may produce a mixed litter of both black and white kittens. White cats are often born with green eyes. Such cats do not conform to the breed standard.

Long-haired White with orange eyes.

Long-Haired Black

This is one of the oldest of the established breeds. The coat should be a dense black—'lustrous raven black' in the words of the English standard. The eyes should be copper or deep orange with no trace of a green rim. It is impossible to tell whether a black kitten will make a good show cat for they are rarely a good color and often gray or rusty, or may even have a scattering of white hairs; sometimes they have a white undercoat which gives a smoke effect. They will begin to show their adult color at five or six months but often will not look their best until they have their second coat at a year to eighteen months old.

Long-Haired Blue (Blue Persian)

The coat should be a uniform blue with no shading either in the individual hair or overall. The eyes should be deep orange or copper without any trace of green. Kittens often have tabby markings but these disappear with age. They are difficult to breed because the blue factor is recessive.

Long-Haired Cream

The coat should be an even shade of cream, the eyes bright copper or orange. Kittens often show tabby markings on legs and tail but these tend to disappear. Paler coats are preferred but are difficult to breed without the undercoat showing lighter. 'Hot' reddish coats tend to occur and the use of Blue Persians in breeding helps to correct this.

Long-Haired Red

The coat should be a deep rich red without markings but this is difficult to achieve and tabby markings tend to appear in the majority of cases. The eyes should be deep copper.

Above: Long-haired Blue.
Left: Long-haired Cream.

Long-Haired Smoke

The coat should be deep black on the back shading to silver on the sides and flanks. The mask and feet should be black with a silver frill and ear tufts. The undercoat should be white. The eyes should be copper or deep orange. In Britain a Blue Smoke is permissible and counts as a separate breed. The smoke effect is achieved by the undercoat showing through and the cat's beauty is enhanced by the contrast of its 'points' (the dark markings of mask and feet). Kittens are born black and it is some weeks before the undercoat begins to show.

Long-Haired Blue-Cream

The coat should be well divided between the two colors which should be broken into patches. There should be no ticking and the patching must extend to face, legs and tail which should not be solid color. The eyes should be deep copper or orange. In Britain and on the continent of Europe the standard contradicts American requirements which are an even intermingling of colors giving an effect akin to shot silk. Males are exceptionally rare in this breed and if they occur, seldom survive.

Long-Haired Tortoiseshell

The coat should be evenly broken into patches of black, red and cream. The patches should be clearly defined with no mingling of colors and there should be no sign of stripes or tabby markings. The eyes should be deep copper or orange. Males are seldom born and are usually sterile.

Long-Haired Tortoiseshell and White: Calico

The coat should be particolored in even patches of red, cream and black like the tortoiseshell, but there should also be clear white patches, preferably on the chest, face, legs and paws. A white blaze between the eyes from the nose to the top of the head is particularly desirable. The eyes should be deep copper or orange. As with the preceding two mixed-color breeds, males are seldom born.

Long-Haired Silver: Chinchilla

The undercoat should be pure white, and the coat hair on the back, flanks, head and tail tipped with black so that they have a sparkling silver appearance. The legs may be slightly shaded but chin, ear tufts, stomach and chest must be pure white. There should be no sign of tabby markings nor of any cream or brownish tinge. The tip of the nose should be brick red and the visible skin rimming the eyes and lips and the paw pads should be black. Eyes should be round and emerald or blue-green. The bone structure is less heavy than in other long-haired breeds. At one time brown eye colors were allowed, but no longer. Kittens are born with tabby markings but these disappear as the undercoat pushes through. The eye color also improves as the kitten gets older. However, if barring on the legs persists after about ten weeks it is unlikely that it will disappear.

Long-Haired Shaded Silver

This breed, which the British do not recognise, is a Chinchilla with pale silver undercoat instead of white, and heavier ticking. Eyes should be emerald or blue-green.

Long-Haired Brown Tabby

The coat may be of any shade of true brown provided it has no grayish tinge but preference is given to what the British standard calls a 'rich tawny sable'. The ground should make a good contrast with the dense black markings which should follow the standard tabby pattern which consists (to quote the British standard again) of 'delicate pencillings running down the face. The cheeks crossed with two or three distinct swirls. The chest crossed by two unbroken narrow lines, butterfly markings on shoulders. Front of legs striped regularly from toes upwards. The saddle and sides to have deep bands running down them, and the tail to be regularly ringed.' Indistinct or incorrect markings are to be avoided, as is a white tip to the tail. The lips and chin should be the same color as the rings round the eyes but allowance is made for light chins in young cats and kittens. The eyes should preferably be copper but deep copper is also acceptable and the British standard allows hazel. Overall shape should conform to the long-hair type but frequently this breed shows a tendency toward a narrower and longer head with the ears placed too much on top.

Long-Haired Red Tabby

The ground color and markings of the coat should be in a light and deep shade of red. The eyes should be deep copper or deep orange. As with other tabbies a white tip to the tail is undesirable. The 'ginger' or 'marmalade' cat which is a popular pet, would rarely qualify for showing in this breed, for its color is almost always too sandy rather than the deep rich red which the standard requires. Unlike so many breeds the adult markings usually show quite clearly in the kitten, but the same problems of build appear as in the brown tabby.

Long-Haired Silver Tabby

The coat should have a pure silver ground color with dense black markings showing no sign of ticking nor any brown or yellow tinge. Eyes should be green or hazel, and in some American standards blue-green. This is a difficult type to breed. There are the same problems as with the preceding breeds, and it is difficult to produce a distinct tabby pattern.

Long-Haired Blue Tabby

The ground color of the coat, including the lips and chin, should be a pale bluish ivory with fawn overtones which should be more noticeable on the forehead. The markings should be in a deep contrasting blue. The nose should be pink and the eyes deep orange or copper, which is preferred. The Blue Tabby is not recognised by the British Fancy nor by some American associations.

Left: Long-haired Shaded Silver.
Above: Long-haired Brown Tabby.
Right: Long-haired Silver Tabby.

Himalayan

This breed is the result of crossing Siamese with Persian cats. The fur should be long, thick and silky and the body conformation as for other long-hairs, but the coloring should be identical to the points of the Siamese and the eyes should be a deep blue. Attempts to produce a long-haired Siamese before World War II only proved that the Siamese coloring was recessive and the Siamese short-haired coat dominant. But finally a British breeder and an American breeder both independently developed from an accidentally produced Persian with Siamese coloring a true breeding strain which was first officially recognised in the United States in 1957 and in Britain (where the breed is known as Long-Haired Colorpoint) two years earlier.

Khmer

This breed, recognised only in France, is very similar to the Himalayan and requires a Persian coat and conformation with Siamese coloring.

Burman (Sacred Cat of Burma)

The coat should be long and silky but the coloring is similar to that of the Siamese except that the body points should be slightly golden and the paws should be pure white. The eyes should be rich blue. The breed is traditionally that of the temple cats of Burma. At the Temple of Lao-Tsun (the abode of the Gods) there live over a hundred of these cats in which the priests believe the souls of priests are reincarnated. The belief goes back many centuries, to before the time of the Buddha, when the cats were kept as oracles. One venerable old Kittah priest, Mun Ha, and his pure white cat, Sinh, were sitting before the statue of the Goddess Tsun Kyankze seeking guidance and protection against a threatened invasion from Siam, when death suddenly came to him. As the other priests watched in despair, the cat leaped on to the golden throne of Mun Ha and sat upon the head of his dying master. As Sinh faced the golden goddess with sky-blue eyes his golden eyes became sapphire too like hers, his white fur shone with gold and his ears and paws took on the brown of the fertile earth, except for the tips of his

paws where they rested on his master's silver head. As the priests watched, the soul of the holy man passed into the cat, whose eyes turned from the goddess to the door of the temple. The priests understood his gaze, and throwing themselves against the great bronze doors they repelled the first of the invaders. Given heart by the power of the cat, the priests saved the temple from damage and profanation. When they returned Sinh still sat on the throne gazing into the eyes of the goddess. For seven days he did not move and then he died taking the soul of his master from this earth. Seven days later, when the priests met to choose Mun Ha's successor, the cats of the temple, all now changed to the coloring of Sinh, came and surrounded the youngest priest, Lingoa, showing the priests the goddess's choice.

The first cats of this breed to come to the West were a pair sent in 1919 by some priests as a present to Major Gordon Russell, a British soldier living in France, who had helped them escape to Tibet with their sacred cats during a rebellion three years earlier. In 1925 they became an accepted breed in France with their own standards but have only recently been accepted in Britain and the United States.

Shell Cameo

This, and the three following, are recent American breeds developed since 1954 by Dr Rachel Salisbury of Milton Junction, Wisconsin. The name was given because of the appearance of the color combination which was initially the result of crossing Long-hair Tortoiseshell with Smoke. The Shell Cameo should have a pale cream, almost white, undercoat and the fur of the back, flanks, head and tail must be tipped with red to give a delicate shimmer. The face and legs may be lightly tipped but the ear tufts, stomach, chest and chin should be untipped and as pale as possible. There should be no sign of barring or tabby markings. The skin around the eyes and the nose leather should be pink and the eyes golden or copper.

Shaded Cameo

The coat should be a pure red shading from very dark on top to a pale cream on the chin, under the body and under the tail. The legs should match the face coloring. The eyes should be golden or copper and the eye rims and nose leather should be pink.

Smoke Cameo

The coat should be a rich reddish beige with markings in red or a darker beige following the points for the Smoke. The undercoat should be white or pale cream and the ear tufts and ruff, pale cream. The eyes should be golden or copper. Eye rims and nose leather should be pink. There should be no barring or tabby markings.

Tabby Cameo

A pale cream undercoat and ground color with tabby markings in red or beige. The eyes should be golden or copper, the eye rims and nose leather rose.

Peke-Faced Long-Haired Tabby

This breed, which is not recognised outside the United States, should fit the general standards for the Red Long-Haired Cats or the Red Tabby Long-Hairs, but the head should look like that of a Pekinese dog with big round eyes, a pushed-in nose and the ears set wide and low.

Short-haired Breeds

Whilst the long-haired breeds conform to one basic body type, the short-hairs may be divided broadly into the domestic and the foreign breeds. The native American cats, and the British cats from which they originally developed, all have a solid body and rounded head, thick tails and rounded ears, whilst the 'foreign' cats have more lithe, sinuous lines, pointed heads and tapering tails.

Domestic Short-Hair

The color requirements follow those of the long-haired breeds but the British Cat Fancy recognise the following distinct breeds for show purposes: White, Black, Cream, Blue (see British Blue below), Blue-Cream, Silver, Tabby, Red Tabby, Brown Tabby, Tortoiseshell and Tortoiseshell and White. Eye colors should also follow the standards for equivalent coat colors in long-haired cats. The body should be powerfully built with a full chest. Front and back legs should be of equal length and not too high, with neat rounded feet. The head should be rounded with the top of the skull rounded and the cheeks wide and well developed, particularly in stud males. The ears should be set well apart, be medium in size and have rounded tips. The chin should be well developed and in line with the upper lip. The nose should be short but not so short as in long-hairs. The shortish tail should be heavy at the root tapering slightly but ending abruptly. The coat should be short and thick, the hair fine and even in texture with no tendency to wooliness.

British Blue

The coat should be light to medium blue with no trace of tabby markings, shading or white. The large, full eyes should be copper, orange or yellow, with no trace of green.

Chartreux

This is a French breed, very similar to the British Blue. The coat may be any shade of gray or grayish blue. The body is slightly more stocky than the British Blue with a thickset neck; the head should not be quite so round, though the cheeks should be full. The breed is supposed to have been introduced to France by Carthusian monks who brought the cats from South Africa.

Burman kittens.

Manx

The Manx is not simply a cat without a tail. The main characteristics are similar to the domestic short-hairs but the flank should be much deeper than with other breeds and the back legs appreciably longer than the front legs. The back should curve gently from the shoulders to the haunches and the hindquarters should be rounded—'round as an orange' the British standard says. This gives the Manx a peculiar hopping gait rather like a rabbit, a similarity emphasised by the lack of tail which should be complete. Manx are *not* cats which have lost their tails. If you feel the end of a Manx cat's backbone, where in other cats the vertebrae of the tail begin, you will feel a distinct hollow. Some clubs will accept an invisible joint or cartilage in an otherwise perfect specimen but it will, of course, be penalised; and although Manx cats will often produce tailed kittens, only a cat without even a vestigial tail is a true Manx.

The head should be round with prominent cheeks like the domestic short-hairs, but the nose should be longer and the ears longer and pointed.

The coat may be any color but it must be 'double' with a thick, close undercoat and a longer open outer coat, another feature which adds to the rabbity look. The eyes should be large and round and should follow the standard for the color of coat.

Present-day Manx, or 'rumpies' as they are often called, certainly came from the Isle of Man, in the Irish Sea (between Britain and Ireland), and it is possible that the mutation may have originated there, but Manx people tell a number of legends variously suggesting that the original Manx swam ashore from a wrecked ship of the Spanish Armada, a Baltic wreck, or a merchantman trading with the East. There are no tailless cats in Spain, but they are found in Malaya.

How the Manx lost her tail in the first place has been accounted for by the story that she was so late in going into the Ark that Noah, impatient because the waters were rising, slammed the door shut too soon and cut off her tail. Another legend tells how the Manx warriors, seeking to imitate invading Irish who wore plumes in their helmets, took to killing cats to use their bushy tails to decorate their own helmets. One old female cat, determined that her kittens should not be slaughtered for their tails, retired to the top of a mountain to have her next litter and when the kittens were born, bit off their tails and saved their lives. The wise cat passed on her secret and for generations cats bit off their kittens' tails until at last they were born without any.

Although cats use their tails to help their balance, the Manx seems to manage quite happily without one, but the mutation is, in fact, a defect. Manx bred to Manx for more than three generations do not produce live kittens and even those of the third generation are likely to be feeble. The mutation does not only affect the tail but the whole of the spinal column, and vertebrae may be missing elsewhere causing further malformation. The breed is also vulnerable to a malfunction of the sphincter muscles of the anus which can cause problems.

Siamese

Whatever the color, all Siamese breeds have the same basic standards. The body should be of medium size, long and svelte; the males are somewhat bigger than the females. The legs are long and slim, the hind legs slightly higher than the front, and the feet small and oval. The tail is long, thin, even at the root, and tapering to a point. It should not have any kinks though slight kinking at the end is permissible in the British standard. The head should be long and wedge-shaped, tapering smoothly from the large pointed ears (which increase this effect) in a smooth line to the nose. There should be no puffiness to the cheeks and neither should they curve inward which makes the muzzle look too wide and the face pinched. In profile there should be a straight line from above the eyes to the tip of the nose. The chin should not recede as sometimes happens when the upper and lower teeth do not meet properly. Siamese should always have an elegant, sleek appearance, they should never look heavy or fat. The eyes should be almond shaped slanting down toward the nose, and a deep, sapphire color for all breeds. The coat should be short, fine, glossy and close-lying with dark markings known as 'points' on a light body color. The points consist of a dark mask spreading out from the nose and eyes over the cheeks and connected by fine lines to the base of the ears which are also dark; tail, legs and feet should all be densely colored in the same shade. The back is a darker color, though not so dark as the points, becoming paler down the sides and very pale under the belly. Kittens are born almost white and these characteristic points only gradually appear. The link between mask and ears is often lacking until the cat is adult. Many cats have a dark patch on the belly but this is a fault in a show cat, as is any white coloring between the toes. Any brindling of the points is undesirable but this is frequently only temporary and due to illness or very hot weather. As Siamese get older their coat usually becomes darker and show judges make allowance for this.

Seal Pointed Siamese

This was the original coloring of the breed. The coat should be an even color from pale fawn to cream, shading to a lighter, creamy white on the belly and chest. The points should all be a rich seal brown. The pads of the feet and the nose leather should be the same color as the points.

Blue Pointed Siamese

This first Blue Point Siamese was bred in England in 1894. The points should be blue and the body color a glacial white shading gradually into blue on the back, which should be a lighter shade of the cold blue of the points. There should be no sign of fawn in the coloring. The pads of the feet and the nose leather should be slate gray.

Chocolate Pointed Siamese

The original Chocolate Pointed cat was taken from Siam to England in 1897. The body color should be ivory with the points milk chocolate. The pads and nose leather should be a pinky-brown.

Left: British Blue.
Above: Manx.

Lilac Pointed Siamese (*Frost Pointed*)

This comparatively recent breed, which is also known as Frost Point, sometimes occurs in litters where the parents carry both chocolate and blue characteristics; the breed has developed from these cats which always breed true. The coat is frosty gray—almost white—and the points are a lilac gray which has a slight pink tinge. The pads of the feet are pink or mauvish gray and the nose leather should be mauve.

Red Point Siamese (*Red Colorpoint Short-Hair*)

This breed first appeared about 1950 and is still not often found. The points should be a deep red and the body color clear white with shading, if any, in the same tone as the points.

Albino Siamese

The body color should be clean, bright white with the luster common to healthy Siamese. The blue of the blood vessels in the eyes prevent them from being as pink as is usual in other albino animals.

Siamese cats were introduced to Europe from Siam but Thailand was probably not their place of origin. The Siamese is not the common breed there and the Thais often call it the Chinese cat. Wherever it came from, and it was certainly somewhere in the East, it attracted the attention of Siamese royalty who acquired as many cats as they could and began to breed them. We may owe the fixing of the type to Pradgadipok, father of a Siamese king. The cats were highly prized and carefully guarded in his palace. There were dire penalties for stealing them. By 1830 the characteristic features were well established and described in a poem about cats.

It is said that when a member of the royal family died, one of his cats was put into the tomb with him. A small hole was left in the roof through which the cat could escape. When the cat emerged, the priests knew that the soul of the prince had passed into the cat. At the coronation of King Prajadhipok in 1926, a white cat was carried in the procession to the throne room—presumably the soul of the previous king witnessing the accession of his successor.

The first known Siamese cats to reach the West were a pair called Pho and Mia who, in 1884, were given by the royal family to Owen Gould, the English Consul in Bangkok. They were shown at the Crystal Palace the following year and attracted a great deal of attention. That same year two more cats were taken to France and presented to the Jardin des Plantes but it was their great popularity in Britain that quickly established the breed. It was not until 1895 that the first Siamese were imported into the United States, but, as in England, they were immediately popular. There are now many more Siamese cats in the United States than there have ever been in Thailand.

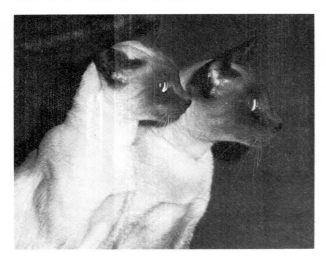

Left: Chocolate Pointed Siamese.
Above: Seal Pointed Siamese.
Right: Blue Pointed Siamese.
Far right: Lilac Pointed Siamese.

The kinky tail which is so common in oriental cats is now considered a fault in the Siamese, but it was once acceptable and so widespread that charming legends grew up to describe its acquisition. One is that an eastern princess, going bathing, removed the rings from her fingers and placed them for safe keeping on the tail of her favorite cat, tying a knot in it to make sure they did not fall off. The tail never quite recovered. Another is that the cat was set to guard a lovely chalice and, fearful lest he fall asleep, twisted his tail around its shaft. For so long did he sit patiently guarding the jeweled cup that when at last he was relieved of his charge, his tail was permanently twisted in proof of his devotion.

Balinese

This breed, recognised by the American Cat Association though not universally accepted, is a long-haired Siamese. That is to say it has Siamese conformation and points but long hair—as opposed to the Colorpoint which is a Persian with Siamese markings. Seal, Blue, Chocolate and Lilac are all accepted, all with blue eyes.

Korat

The general conformation is that of the Siamese but rather more rounded. The coat is solid gray-blue tipped with silver. The eyes should be brilliant green or amber green. This is a breed which genuinely originated in Thailand where it is found only on the Korat Plateau, and highly prized by the local people. According to Jean L. Johnson, who spent six years in Thailand without being able to obtain one, they are virtually impossible to buy and 'given only to the highest officials as a token of esteem and affection'. However, in 1959, after Mrs Johnson had left Thailand, Siamese friends managed to obtain both a male and female which they sent to her in the United States, where they have bred successfully.

Burmese

The Burmese is a little smaller than the typical Siamese and although it has the same foreign shape, all the Siamese characteristics are softened. The head is more rounded, avoiding the chiseled look of the Siamese, the ears are less prominent, the muzzle less sharp and the tail not so thin. The coat should be fine, close-lying, and very glossy; the color an overall rich brown shading to a barely noticeable lighter shade on the underparts. There should be no other

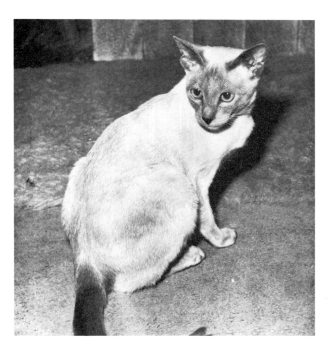

shading or markings of any kind though the British standard does permit faint Siamese-type points provided there is no decided contrast between them and the body color. Young cats and kittens may show slight tabby markings but these usually disappear. The eyes, round in shape (again the British standard permits an almond-shaped Siamese look), should be rich yellow to gold.

A Blue Burmese has now been developed which is like the brown in every respect except the color, which should be a bluish-gray shading to a pale brown or gray on the belly.

The Burmese did have its origin in Burma, but the present breed is not the natural type. In 1930, Dr Joseph C. Thompson of San Francisco, imported from Burma a female brown cat of foreign type called Wong Mau. Since there was no brown male available, she was mated with a Siamese and from their litter geneticists at Harvard produced the present breed. It is not surprising that the Siamese characteristics still show through, particularly in Europe where the first Burmese was imported into Britain in 1947. In France, the breed is known as the Zibeline.

Abyssinian

The Abyssinian is of foreign body type with fine bones and long, lithe lines, but it should strike a balance between the cobby type and the svelte Siamese. The feet are small and round, the head is long and pointed but gently rounded. The ears are pointed but not so large as in the Siamese, and the tail not so long and thicker at the root. The coat of the Abyssinian is unlike any other. The fur should be soft and silky with a fine sheen, but thick and springy. Each hair should be ticked with two or three bands of black or dark brown separated by lighter bands of ruddy brown. A darker color is permissible along the spine provided that the hairs are fully ticked and the tail and ears should be tipped with black. The underside and inside of the forelegs, which are lighter, should harmonise with the main body color with not more than single ticking on each hair. They should preferably be unmarked, orange-brown.

Left: Blue Burmese.
Below: Brown Burmese.

78

The paw pads should be black, as should be the lower part of the hind legs. The nose leather should be red. The large, expressive eyes should be almond-shaped and either green, gold or hazel in color.

There is also a Red Abyssinian strain with a copper red coat ticked with a darker color and with the tail and ears tipped in dark brown. With this variety the underside should be a deep apricot and the paw pads and nose leather should be pink.

Like the Siamese, the Abyssinian is not the common breed of the country from which it gets its name, yet it was from Abyssinia that the first was taken to Europe. The wife of a British officer, Mrs Lennard, took one to England in 1869, though the breed was not exhibited at the Crystal Palace Show until 1883 and they did not appear in the United States until the 1930s.

In shape the Abyssinian looks very like the domestic cat of ancient Egypt as you can see by comparing it with some of the surviving paintings. Although the present American and European cat is the result of British breeding, it appears to have both the African wildcat, *Felis lybica,* and another African wildcat, *Felis ocreata,* in its ancestry.

Russian Blue

The Russian Blue has a 'foreign' shape. It should be fine boned and elegant with long legs and neat, oval feet, large, pointed ears, a long nose (though not so long as a Siamese), long neck, a receding forehead and almond eyes. It has a softer line than the Siamese and this is partly due to the coat which distinguishes it from all other cats. The fur should be short and thick and very fine. It should not lie flat but stand up with the soft texture and silky sheen of velvet plush. Color should be a bright, even blue, with no sign of tabby markings and no shading. In the United States light or lavender blue is preferred, but in Europe medium to dark shades are required. The eyes should be a vivid green, though in kittens and young cats they will appear yellow.

'Russian' is a comparatively recent name for this breed which used to be known as the

Abyssinian cat and Abyssinian kitten.

Archangel cat and was supposedly taken to England by British seamen who first sailed the trade route between England and Russia's northern port on the Barents Sea in the time of Elizabeth I. The Scandinavian countries have produced some excellent specimens of this breed but the genuineness of its northern origins is confused by the use in the past of the name Maltese for cats with a blue coat.

Havana Brown (Chestnut Brown)

Another fine-boned foreign type, the Havana must have a sleek and glossy coat in a rich, warm brown without markings or white spots. Even the whiskers should be of the same color. Body and tail should be medium long and in proportion to each other. The ears should be round-tipped, the legs slim with the hind legs slightly longer, the feet oval with pinkish-brown pads, the lips and nose leather brown. The eyes should be almond in shape and from chartreuse to dark green in color; darker greens are preferred.

Kittens are born the same color as they will be when adult, but occasionally show slight shading or tabby markings when changing their coat.

The Havana is one of the newest breeds. It was developed in Britain and first shown in the United States in 1959.

Bald Cats

Hairlessness, like the Rex coat, is caused by a recessive gene. An American breed known as the Mexican hairless cat has now disappeared. It had big ears and a bare tail, but was not completely bald since it had a smooth short coat like a Boxer dog—or a rat, which it looked unpleasantly like. This mutation crops up from time to time and in recent years hairless cats have been resuscitated in France by Professor Etienne Letard. A pair of Siamese regularly produced hairless offspring among their litters and when he mated them together they were found to breed true. The kittens are not born completely bald but have a few light hairs which fall away after weaning, leaving only a slight downy fuzz. The mutation has also been fixed by breeders in Canada who have claimed it as a new breed which they have called the 'Sphynx'.

Quite apart from their strange appearance, these 'bald' cats are extremely sensitive to cold.

Maine Coon Cat

This wildcat is believed to be descended from long-haired tabbies that became feral after their introduction by early settlers. It is large and powerfully built with fur of about the same length as a raccoon and, when it has the right kind of markings, it does show some resemblance to

Left: Russian Blue.
Above: Havana Brown.

it, but there is absolutely no truth in the belief that the breed is the result of crossing a cat and a raccoon. Such a hybrid is not possible; the raccoon does not belong to the cat family but is more closely related to dogs—though not closely enough to breed with them either.

Rex

The distinguishing mark of the Rex is its coat which lacks some of the types of hair which make up the coats of other cats. There are two kinds: the English Rex, which has only down hairs, and the German Rex, which has a combination of awned down hairs and down hairs. Both produce a wavy coat, but the hair of the German Rex becomes straight shortly before reaching full adulthood and then regains its waviness. Rex fur occurs in other animals, especially in rabbits where it has been systematically bred, and although it is caused by a single recessive gene, it could be introduced into any breed of cat including long-hairs. This breed was developed after the English cat expert Sidney Denham discovered a curly coated kitten born of a tortoiseshell and an unknown father in Cornwall. The owner agreed to collaborate in a scheme of systematic breeding so that the mutation could be fixed.

The kittens are born curly and the whiskers and eyebrows are also wavy. The coat is particularly fine and silky and it would be possible to breed out the wave whilst retaining the fine coat, as has already been done with Rex-coated rabbits.

Above: Rex cat, this is a coat type rather than a breed.
Top Left: Van cat and kitten. These white and auburn cats come from eastern Turkey and are natural swimmers. They have been introduced into Britain and America and given full breed status by the Cat Fancy.
Left: The Scottish Fold, a genuine drop-eared cat which has been artificially bred from mutations. Kittens do not have the distinctive drop ears which develop when they are older. This confused the judges at a British Show in 1971 and although the breed is not recognized a young cat won a prize.

Choosing a Cat

You probably have a cat already, but if you are thinking of acquiring one for the first time, or of giving one as a present, or even of providing an existing pet with a companion, it is worth considering carefully what cat to get and even whether you should get one at all.

There are two obvious questions. Why do you want a cat and how much attention are you prepared to give it? If you want a pet to match the furnishings, buy a china cat. If you want an animal to protect your property, then get a dog, and a big one—though a cat of mine did once attack a friend already known to her when I gave him a key to the apartment while I was out. If you are giving a cat as a present make absolutely sure that it will be welcome and will be properly cared for, and if it is a present for a child, be sure that the recipient's parents are prepared to look after and welcome it or there will be an unhappy cat. Are you sure you want a cat, and not a playful kitten? Too many people, captivated by a kitten's antics, have no time for the older animal which is cruelly cast out unwanted. If you give a cat the right amount of care and attention, it will amply return your affection and interest, and even in its sedate maturity retain a great deal of its kittenish quality.

What Kind of Cat?

Some cats just arrive. Strays who decide they like your home and you and, given any encouragement, move in. Sometimes friends or neighbors have a cat in litter and kittens looking for a home. In either case, any feelings about a particular breed will probably be overruled by the presence of the cat itself, but if you are looking for a cat, try first to decide which breed will be happiest in your home. Remember that all the long-hairs need regular daily grooming. They tend to be somewhat less active than short-hairs, but this will vary from cat to cat. The Siamese, Burmese and Abyssinian are active and friendly but consequently need human company. The Siamese in particular enjoy carrying on a conversation and being involved in every activity. Some people find their meow and that of the Burmese unpleasant and when a Siamese female is on heat her raucous calling can be extremely disturbing. The Burmese seems to have a somewhat calmer temperament than the Siamese, who can be very neurotic if left alone for long periods. If you choose a Siamese and wish to leave the cat alone all day it would be better to have two cats to keep each other company. Both Siamese and Abyssinian take more readily to a lead than other breeds.

However, personality is no more the result of shape and color than it is with human beings. It is much more a question of upbringing, both the early training by the kitten's mother and the influence of the personality and conduct of the owner. One long-haired black bundle belonging to a friend whose apartment I once shared was far from placid, in fact she was positively schizophrenic, suddenly rushing off to fight a shadow, demanding reassurance at the most unlikely times, spending ten minutes saying 'thank you' before starting to eat a meal, timid of strangers until she had sized them up but throwing herself at the door whenever she heard me or her owner coming home. But then her owner was just as neurotic and unpredictable—and everybody found them both quite adorable!

I do not think that there is any particular breed that gets on better with other animals. This again is a matter of the individual cat's personality and the way in which the household treats them all.

If you choose a pedigree kitten you can be sure what shape and color of cat it will grow up to be and will have some indication of the way its character might develop, but a non-pedigree cat can be an equally affectionate and entertaining companion and it is very rare to find any well-cared-for cat that is not beautiful.

Kitten or Cat?

Cats are very clean animals and by the time a kitten is old enough to leave its mother she will have made sure that it is house-trained and taught to wash itself, so you need not be afraid that a kitten will make a mess of your home as, for instance, a young puppy might. You will have to take more care over a kitten's food, keep a closer watch on its health and give it much more time than an adult cat, but there is nothing more fascinating than watching, and helping, a kitten discover itself, invent games and explore the world, thereby establishing a relationship with the animal, which is more difficult to achieve with a cat that is already mature. It is also easier to introduce a young kitten into a household where there are already other cats or dogs.

But a kitten is a delicate little creature and easily injured. You must be prepared to take good care of it and if you have young children who might not realise how carefully it must be handled, it might be better to choose a slightly older cat. Cats are usually remarkably fond of children and will put up with treatment from them that they would not tolerate from a grown-up, but a kitten is not so capable of looking after itself. Cats have a remarkable ability to land on their feet, but they do need sufficient distance in which to right themselves and a kitten dropped from a small child's arms could easily damage its back.

An adult cat will be more set in its ways; you may not be able to train it to do things in quite the way you want and you may have to devise a working compromise. If a stray has chosen to make its home with you, it presumably thinks you suit its way of life, and if you think of adopting a friend's cat you will know enough about it to decide whether it will fit happily into your home. An adult from a pet shop is less predictable, but all cats respond to care and affection however independent they sometimes appear to be.

Finding a Cat

Many people obtain a cat because they know of someone with a litter of kittens needing homes, and the cat shelters of the animal protection societies always have unwanted kittens which they are happy to give away to save them from being destroyed. If neither of these sources is easily available, you should be able to buy a non-pedigree cat quite cheaply from a pet shop.

If you want a pedigree cat you must be prepared to pay quite a lot for it. You will get some idea of how much from advertisements and listings in pet magazines and local papers. If you buy direct from the breeder, you will probably have to pay more but you will get a more valuable cat because the breeders usually sell their best animals direct. Although there are some large catteries run as commercial undertakings, most breeders raise cats as a hobby, not a business, and if you can buy your cat from a small-scale breeder of this kind you will probably be able to find out much more about the way the cat may develop from the character of the cat's close relatives and the way the breeder treats the animals.

I think the ideal way of selecting a cat is to find a breeder whose cats you like and ask to be informed when a new litter is expected. Ask to visit to see the kittens as soon as their eyes are open and, if the breeder will permit it, call several times before the litter is ready to leave their mother. Kittens reveal their character much more clearly when set against their siblings. You will probably find that you will not have to make the difficult choice between one kitten and another, but that one of them will choose you. If you are looking for two cats to keep each other company you will be able to see which have already become particular playmates who will be happy together.

This makes a lot of extra trouble for the breeder and you may have to choose a kitten on a single visit, but it is worth a try, particularly if the breeder is raising cats in his own home.

To find a breeder you should consult the advertisements in your local newspaper or ask the advice of the local veterinarian, or you could visit a cat show at which your local breeders would be exhibiting.

Male or Female?

This really is not the difficult decision it sounds, for if you want a cat as a pet and do not intend to breed you should have your pet neutered and then there is very little difference in temperament, although a male will be somewhat larger in some breeds. If you intend to breed, then get a female, for unless you intend to set up a full-scale cattery with quarters for the cats outside the house, you will find the mature male's habit of spraying urine to mark his territory obnoxious. You may be able to train a male never to spray indoors but even outside the odor can be unpleasantly lingering. Unneutered males are also more inclined to fight which could lead to extra veterinary bills for treating wounds. You would be better to keep a female only and take her to stud when she is in season. There is no truth in the suggestion that it is 'kinder' to let a female have one litter before having her spayed; but if you are sure of homes for her kittens, the birth and bringing up of a litter is beautiful to observe.

Which Kitten?

You must try to suppress all those compassionate feelings that well up when you see a sad and sickly kitten crouched in the corner of a pet shop or hiding away from the rest of a boisterous litter. Unless you want to face endless difficulties and possible heartbreak when the little creature finally succumbs you should look for the fittest of the litter. Runny noses, watery eyes or scaly eyelids could all be danger signs, dirty ears may be an indication of mites, bald patches in the fur of ringworm. A soiled patch under the tail is an indication of diarrhea which may be caused by internal disorders. There are a number of minor ailments and parasites to which kittens are subject and they can all be cured or cleared, but you will not want to start out with a kitten suffering from them. Excessive dandruff and black specks in the fur are signs of fleas. If you have children in the house it is essential that the cat has recently been 'wormed', that is disinfested from internal parasites, for some of them can be passed on to man. The drugs used can be very strong and this should be done under a veterinarian's control.

A reputable breeder or pet dealer will not want to sell you a sick cat and will readily agree to accept the animal back if a veterinarian does not give it a clean bill of health. In fact the breeder may well consider himself a better person than you to effect the cure. It is certainly worth taking a new kitten for a thorough medical checkup, and then at the same time it can be immunised against feline enteritis.

It is difficult to imagine a kitten that is not enchanting and even those which are clearly sick make the cat lover long to rescue them — but when choosing a new kitten you must exclude compassion and look for a strong healthy animal.

Welcoming the New Cat

Always collect a new cat at a time when you can give it plenty of attention. If you work, then leave it until the beginning of the weekend—though if you have a house full of boisterous children it may be better to bring the kitten home at some quieter time so that it can get a little used to its new surroundings and you before having to cope with the noise and excitement of a lot of other people.

Take a towel or blanket to wrap the kitten in; this will be cosy and comforting and at the same time protect you from scratches if the animal gets frightened. If you have to go any distance you would do well to buy a carrying box or basket, and if you are collecting the cat by car and have no one to hold it while you drive, a box will be essential. For this purpose and later for the occasional trip to the veterinarian, a cardboard box—specially made with air holes and carrying handles—will be quite adequate and can be obtained cheaply from a veterinarian or pet store, but if you are likely to want to take your cat on frequent journeys a wickerwork basket will not be expensive and will last for many years, or one made of fiberglass will be light to carry and easily cleaned and disinfected.

There is always a warm welcome for a new kitten — but make sure that it is a sensible welcome and that its needs have been anticipated, including a toilet tray.

Even if you eventually intend to let your cat out of the house you must equip yourself with a sanitary pan and cat litter for as a small kitten it has almost certainly been trained by its mother to use a pan, and until it is settled in its new home you should not let it out. A plastic or enamel tray about eighteen inches square with sides about three inches high will be ideal. You may use sand, ash or sawdust as litter but you will find one of the proprietary cat litters will absorb both moisture and odor more efficiently. A small sieve trowel will be useful to remove solid wastes and hardened lumps of litter, enabling you to replenish the litter rather than replace it entirely. But make sure that it is kept clean or the cat may refuse to use it and make a mess elsewhere. Of course, if the kitten is frightened or excited it may forget itself. If it does, or if you have a very young kitten that has not been properly trained you will soon be able to guess when it needs to go to the toilet for an expression of unease and discomfort will spread across its face. Lift the kitten up and place it in the box. If it fails to cover its dirt you can take its forepaws and dig a hole in the litter—the kitten will soon get the idea. One word of warning, if you have an open fire, be careful not to leave cold ashes in the fireplace, for understandably the cat may imagine this is a second toilet place.

You will need a brush and open-toothed comb for grooming, and a pair of nail clippers for cutting claws. If you are going to let the cat out you will need a collar to carry an identification tag. Make sure you get the special kind made for cats with one section slightly elastic so that if the collar gets caught on a hook or branch the cat can escape. If you intend to walk your cat then you will also need a leash and may prefer a special cat harness rather than a collar; most cats seem to like them better.

Your new kitten will also need a bed. The box or basket in which you collect it may serve if the kitten can climb in and out. Line the bottom with newspaper and put a rumpled piece of blanket on top. A hot water bottle under the blanket will keep it warm and act as a substitute for the warmth of its mother and the rest of the litter. After a time a cat will choose its own place to sleep but at first you must provide a cosy nest. Do not put it on the floor where there may be draughts, place it on a low table or a trunk.

Being separated from its mother and taken to entirely new surroundings is quite a frightening experience for a little kitten. Treat it very gently, try to avoid sudden movements and loud noises, make sure it is warm, comfort and encourage it. Always have fresh water available and if it seems too upset to eat put a little food on your finger so that the kitten can suck or lick it off. Ask the breeder or dealer what food the kitten has been used to and provide the same, even if you intend to feed it quite differently later. You can gradually introduce changes in its diet.

If you already have a dog or another cat you will have to keep a watch to see that neither hurts the other. Make sure that you give the earlier pet plenty of attention so that neither gets jealous. Do not feed them together until the have got used to each other. In fact many dogs and most cats will accept and take care of a small kitten and you may find the greatest problem is to stop the kitten from pestering the older animal. With an older cat the difficulties may be greater.

Your new pet will want some toys. A table tennis ball, or one of the toy mice that pet shops sell would be fun for your cat, but a crumpled piece of paper and a piece of string will keep it as happy as anything.

Looking After a Kitten

Your cat will almost certainly have been weaned before it leaves its mother but should you take on a very young orphan you will have to look after it just like a human baby. Occasionally a mother cat will lose interest in her kittens and then they must be hand-reared too.

First, you will have to feed it. Cat's milk is made up quite differently from cow's milk, it has a far higher protein content; many grown cats cannot stomach cow's milk and it is certainly not suitable for a tiny kitten. Unless you are lucky enough to find a foster mother you will have to make up an equivalent kind of milk. Your veterinarian will probably have his own formula, but a cup of homogenised vitamin D milk into which is beaten 1 egg yolk, 1 teaspoon of lime water (which helps bone formation) and 2 teaspoons of dextrose will make an adequate substitute. At first a kitten needs five feeds a day of about two teaspoonfuls each, given at two-hour intervals. The feed must be given at a temperature of about 101·5°F. Put the feeding bottle into hot water until it reaches the right temperature and test it on your wrist as you would a baby's bottle. A normal baby's bottle may have too big a teat, a doll's bottle might do the job better, or if that still does not work, a twist of clean cloth (a handkerchief will do) can be dipped in the milk and given to the kitten to suck. You should burp the kitten like a human baby, but unlike humans you will also have to help it to get rid of its wastes. A mother cat massages her kitten's belly with her tongue; you can use a sponge or a rough towel dipped in warm water rubbing always towards the hindquarters. This will help the kitten to urinate and defecate. You must then clean the kitten carefully. You must do this regularly until the kitten can manage without your help. Gradually you can increase the amount given at each feed and space them further apart.

The kitten's eyes will open during its second week, but it will not have got used to using them until it is two weeks old and it cannot cope with bright lights until it is four weeks old. Like a human baby, its eyes sometimes stick together. Gently rub the eyes from the nose outward with a pad of wool soaked in warm borax solution until you have removed the secretion and then dry them carefully. If the eyes seem late in opening, the same treatment followed by a smear of white petroleum jelly should help.

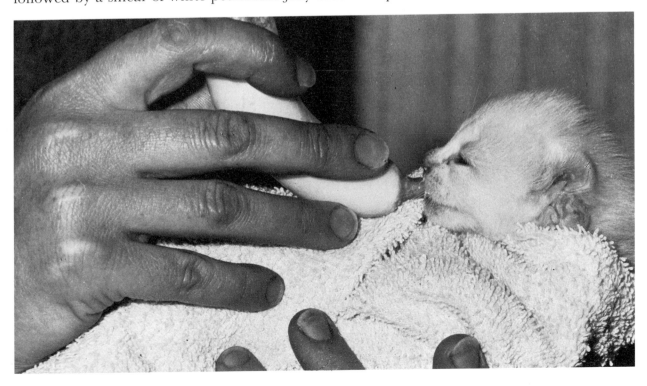

If you have to nurse an orphan kitten a doll's bottle or a syringe will help you feed it, but a mother's natural milk is always preferable.

To sex a kitten you should carefully inspect its hindquarters. Below the tail you will see the anus, which appears circular, and about three-eighths of an inch below it the rudimentary testicles of the male. In females the vagina shows as a small slit close to the anus. It is easiest to sex kittens before their coat begins to grow.

A cat has twenty-six teeth which begin to appear during its second week, but it will be a month or more before all are through. When it is about six months old it will lose these milk teeth and its adult teeth will push through.

At about three weeks the kitten will begin to struggle out of its box and it is time to introduce it to a sanitary pan. This is also the time to begin to wean the kitten.

All this a mother cat will normally do, much better than any human substitute. If the mother is happy and able to supply her kitten's demands, you can delay weaning until the kitten is five weeks old, but not later. To begin with, a mixture like that given as substitute milk will serve. One of the powdered baby milk foods could also be used, with a little lime and dextrose added. Do not give more than one teaspoonful a day at first, increasing this after the first week.

If a kitten is still feeding from its mother this is only a supplement to its diet. You can go on from this to baby cereals (or you may be able to obtain a special cereal prepared for kittens) which should be given mixed with a little warm milk or diluted evaporated milk. Next begin to introduce some solid food, cooked white fish, scraped raw beef, raw or scrambled eggs. Until the kitten's teeth are well established you will need to mash or chop all the food, and always remove all the bones. By eight weeks old the kitten should be fully weaned and eating four varied meals a day. Meat is essential—an all fish diet can result in a skin disease. Most cats will enjoy breakfast cereal mixed with their food, or a small amount of rice pudding with a little evaporated milk. You can try a little cow's milk at this point, but it may cause diarrhea and some cats never like it. Always have fresh water available. Cats get thirsty and milk is a *food*, not a drink. A little liquid magnesia added to milk foods will help avoid digestive troubles and a few drops of halibut oil will prevent rickets.

Feeding Your Cat

By six months old a cat will only need two meals a day and when it is fully grown it can manage quite well on one big one—though it may persist in demanding two. Its adult needs will be from four to seven ounces of food per day. Try to keep mealtimes regular, for cats are creatures of habit, and if a cat rejects a particular meal do not leave it about to collect dirt and flies.

In the natural state the cat is carnivorous: it eats meat, but a continuous diet of a single kind of meat will not give the cat all it needs—unless you care to provide a supply of small birds or rodents where it can eat the whole carcass! There is no need to buy expensive foods, though if a cat gets a taste for turkey breast and smoked salmon it may turn up its nose at a more plebeian menu. My own cats thrive on a diet that consists of chicken giblets, boned rabbit, cheap white fish, a varied range of canned cat foods (some of which include a quantity of cereal) supplemented by part of whatever I happen to be eating if it is something they like. They will go to any lengths to steal a little smoked salmon or dressed crab. One of them has developed a passion for spaghetti and another for dates! Butter, cheesecake and all kinds of things will turn them into thieves—they have even been caught making off with a doughnut or half a loaf. When one of them discovered a way of opening the freezer door almost nothing was safe.

Cats get up to all kinds of tricks and can be easily trained. This cat has his own catch to open the door.

A titbit occasionally, even if it is something not really good for them, will do no harm, but if a cat persistently pesters or steals from the table it must be firmly disciplined, for once permitted, it is a habit that will prove difficult to eradicate. It is *not* sufficient to feed a cat on human left-overs, nor is it sufficient to allow a cat only to eat things that it likes. Despite all old tales to the contrary, a cat will not necessarily choose a balanced diet of what is best for it. It is up to the owner to make sure that it gets a proper proportion of proteins, fats, carbo-hydrates, minerals and vitamins. It is essential that a cat get an adequate supply of vitamin A, for unlike all other animals cats cannot synthesise it. Raw liver, milk and cheese are some sources of Vitamin A. Failing them 2–4 drops of a proprietary Vitamin A preparation should be added to the food daily, according to age.

The diet you plan will probably depend on how much you can budget, but muscle and organ meats, fowl, fish, cheese, egg yolk, small quantities of green vegetables and mashed potatoes can all play a part. There is always controversy as to whether a cat's food should be cooked or raw. Pork should always be well cooked since cats are as susceptible as man to the parasites it can carry. Fish too should be cooked unless it is really fresh. Research on a diet consisting only of meat and milk showed cats thrived better if it was uncooked—but since this was a limited diet the result cannot be considered conclusive. For the rest it is up to you and the cat, but *never* give it meat or other food straight from the freezer. Proprietary dried foods, which most cats like, are a useful stand-by when food has to be left out and for the occasion when the cat's dinner unaccountably gets left off the shopping list. If your cat does not have access to outdoor grass you should grow a pot indoors. Special quick-growing strains have been developed which you may be able to get from your pet shop—or plant some oat seeds and put them in a sunny corner. Cats eat grass as an emetic to clear fur balls and for a purge; according to the experts it is not digested. Nevertheless, I have a cat that likes grass so much that it has to be kept out of reach except for a short nibble each day.

Cats like to gnaw on bones, but make sure they are large and not brittle. Never give a cat meat or fish containing small bones. They can easily get lodged in the throat or even pierce the gum or cheek. If a bone, or any other object, does get lodged reassure the cat that you are helping it and carefully inspect the mouth. Gently remove the object. You may have to pull quite hard but do not jerk or you may tear the flesh or do other damage. If a fish bone is wedged and you cannot easily dislodge it you may be able to cut the bone with a pair of blunt-ended scissors and then extract each piece.

Grooming Your Cat

Cats are fastidious animals and keep themselves scrupulously clean, but they all need a little help and long-hairs must be groomed at least once daily. When a cat 'washes' itself it is not only swilling off dirt, it is scrubbing and combing with the rough surface of its tongue. Cats also use licking to dry themselves when they get wet, to smooth down rumpled fur and to spread a film of saliva over themselves to increase heat loss in very hot weather. Their tongues are so long and flexible that they can reach every part of their bodies except the head, the back of the neck and between the shoulder blades. They reach these places by moistening their front paws and using them as face cloths. If you have two cats you will find them washing these inaccessible places for each other. In the process, they swallow a quantity of fur which collects

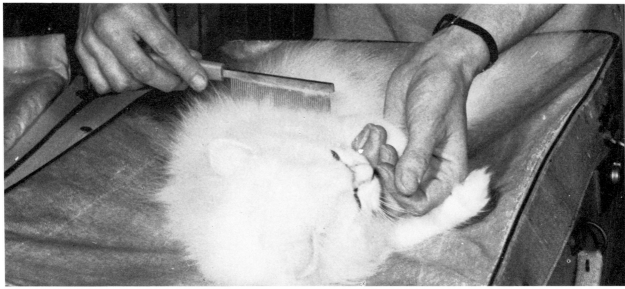

Joseph **(above)**, the heavy-weight tabby, weighs in at forty-eight pounds. He has no intention of dieting either, for his late owner left a bequest to ensure that he will eat well for the rest of his life. **Left:** Cat burglar.

in the stomach and is regurgitated as hair balls. If fur passes beyond the stomach into the intestine it can cause a blockage. If the cat is off its food and appears to have a distended stomach this may be the trouble and you should consult your vet. A few drops of mineral oil given each week, or a dab of petroleum jelly on the nose which the cat will then lick off, may help to prevent the formation of balls and pass the hair straight through. (But do not use carbolated petroleum jelly which is poisonous to cats.) Regular grooming is a much better preventive, and will stop so much hair getting on your carpets and upholstery. Short-hairs should be combed and then briskly brushed with a stiff hairbrush. A final smoothing down with a piece of velvet or a silk handkerchief will help produce a fine gloss on the coat and is particularly recommended if you intended to enter the cat in a show.

Long-haired cats need more thorough treatment at least once a day, and probably more often during the spring moult. First, remove all loose hair with a coarse comb and try to tease out any knots. Matted fur, which may have built up around a twig or burr, must be broken up (if through your neglect it is a solid mass you will have to cut it out with scissors). Then give the whole coat a thorough brushing, giving particular attention to the tail and ruff. If

Archbishop **(above)** is an even more formidable contender, tipping the scales at thirty-three pounds. Pet of the residents at an old folk's home in Edinburgh, Scotland, he is ten years old and has put his live mousehunting days behind him.
Right: Alcoholic?

you still feel the fur looks dirty you can sprinkle the coat with good-quality talcum powder which should first be combed into the coat and then thoroughly brushed out. Alternatively, your pet shop may recommend a safe dry shampoo specially for cats. If you are showing a long-haired cat, you should carry out this intensive grooming for at least a month before the show, but do not powder on the day of the show for if any talcum is left in the coat the cat might be disqualified.

Most cats enjoy being brushed, but with a kitten or a timid cat let the animal play with the brush first to reassure it that there is nothing to fear. Vacuuming has also been recommended as a good way of removing dead hair, and perhaps some cats enjoy it. A vacuum is one of the few things of which the cats that I have owned have been terrified, but it is certainly worth trying.

Your cat may collect a small amount of fluid in the corner of its eyes which dries and cakes on the muzzle, or a small excretion may develop to prevent damage from a hair that has gone into the eye. This should be wiped away with a piece of moist cotton or a soft tissue. If the eyes are continually watering you should see a vet.

A specially made scratching post **(left)** will save wear and tear on your carpets and furniture. You will find friendly help at your local veterinarian or animal clinic.

Cats are always finding their way into holes and corners where dirt collects, and find difficulty in cleaning it from the inside of the ear. Again, this can be carefully wiped away with a moist cotton pad.

A cat that lives its life indoors will sharpen its claws upon your furniture unless you provide a rough log or a piece of wood covered with old rug to serve as a scratching post (you can also buy them ready-made from a pet shop). The cat is not actually sharpening its claws but in the case of its front paws removing the worn-out outer sheath to reveal the sharp new claw beneath (it bites the sheath off the back claws) and generally exercising the claws' retractile muscles. Without the wear and tear of outdoor life the claws may also grow too long and should be trimmed with a pair of nail clippers. The kind that look like a small pair of gardener's secateurs are the easiest to use. If you cradle the cat in the crook of your arm and hold the paw firmly, gently squeezing the claw out of its sheath, you will find it quite simple. You may find it helpful to have someone else distract and soothe the cat until it gets used to it, or even to have someone else hold the cat while you do the trimming. The claws are translucent and you should position yourself so that the light shines through them and you can easily see the pink area in the claw which is the quick. You must not cut back into this. If in doubt, cut well clear, since it is better to have to trim the claws more frequently than to put the cat in pain.

Your Cat's Health

Most cats are sturdy, healthy creatures but they are susceptible to a number of diseases which every cat owner should know how to recognise. However, except for minor ailments and injuries it is unwise to try to treat the cat yourself. Take it along to the veterinarian if you suspect there is something wrong and he will tell you what treatment is required. In case of accident carry out the necessary first aid but get the animal to the veterinarian or vice versa as soon as possible. If private veterinary treatment is beyond your means you will find that veterinary colleges will be happy to treat your pet without making any charge. If you are not lucky enough to have a college in your area most cities have an animal clinic run by one of the welfare societies which will provide treatment free or for whatever contribution you can afford.

George **(left)** has learned to use the knocker, but if you want your pet to come and go as he pleases you can fit a self-closing door flap. But be warned that if he wants to entertain it will let his friends in too!
Writer Ernest Hemingway **(below)** with his cat and painter Henri Matisse **(bottom)** with his pet, Gros Chat.

Diseases

The most dangerous cat diseases are feline infectious enteritis, pneumonitis and feline viral rhinotracheitis (FVR). All are highly infectious. Vaccines are now available which will protect your cat against these killers. They should be administered as soon as the kitten is old enough to leave its mother and booster shots given at the necessary intervals.

Fever, loss of appetite, vomiting, listlessness and a refusal to drink water are all indications of feline enteritis. Cats are most susceptible between four and six months of age, and in a great many cases it proves fatal. If older than eighteen months they usually survive if they are given treatment in time.

A high temperature, running eyes and nose, sneezing and coughing, loss of weight and loss of appetite may indicate pneumonitis or FVR. Their development is much slower than feline enteritis. The first things you would notice would be the runny nose and eyes which would persist for a week at least and possibly several. If the disease attacks an otherwise healthy cat it will respond to treatment in the majority of cases. If you suspect any of these scourges seek expert advice. Do not take your pet to the veterinarian's office unless he asks you to do so, for you run the risk of transmitting the disease to other cats.

Humorous photographs, like this student rodent catcher taken by British photographer Mable Oliver, were popular as postcards and sold thousands of copies in the early years of this century. But cats do not need props or trick photographs to bring you countless hours of interest and amusement.

Cats can suffer from many of the same diseases as man: tuberculosis, cystitis, anemia, leukemia, cancer, rabies and diabetes for instance. You would not expect to diagnose or treat tuberculosis or cancer in your family, and similarly you should not expect to be your own cat's physician. But you should learn to recognise the symptoms of ill health.

A general loss of appetite is often a first sign that something is wrong. The closing or partial closing of the nictitating membrane (the cat's extra eyelid which closes upwards from the inside of the eye) is another signal—unless you know your cat has been eating an excessive amount of grasshoppers, which for some unknown reason also causes this to happen. A reddened tip to the tongue may mean a virus infection. Sneezing with a discharge is a serious sign, although like us a cat will sneeze to clear its passages or because of dust. Yellow- or ivory-looking gums and eyelids, which should usually be pink, may indicate anemia or a liver disorder. Excessive scratching may indicate some form of parasite. An unusual lump may be only a temporarily inflamed gland but it could also be an indication of a serious abscess or of a cancerous growth.

Parasites

The most common is the flea. There are cat fleas, dog fleas and human fleas—but if the appropriate animal is not about they will make do with one of the others. However careful breeders are, and however flea-free their mothers, new kittens somehow often manage to pick them up. Their favorite places are around the head and ears, the back of the neck, the rump and the tail, but check all over. The best way to get rid of them is simply to pick them off. If there are flea eggs on the cat or in its bedding or anywhere in the house you may get a further infestation. If you treat the cat with a remedial powder it will shake some of it onto the places with which it comes in contact and kill off any eggs that may be hatching out. If you use a powder, or one of the sprays or baths which are also marketed, follow the instructions carefully and *never* use a powder containing DDT. When you buy a preparation read the instructions *in the store*. I know that very often powders are bought with the storekeeper's recommendation which have been clearly labeled 'Not to be used on cats'.

Ticks are small parasites which suck blood so that their bodies swell up. They attach themselves very firmly so that the head burrows beneath the cat's skin and should be removed by pressing with a small piece of cotton (or a cotton-tipped stick) dipped in ether or alcohol. This will make them release their grip and they can then be lifted clear and should be burned immediately. If your cat should suffer from a serious infestation take it to the vet who will be able to give it a dip which will remove the parasites.

Lice can also attack a cat. Even if you can remove them they will leave their eggs behind, so consult your vet for the appropriate treatment.

Mites cause two common cat diseases: mange and canker. A cat with mange will scratch and rub the areas where these burrowing parasites make tunnels under the skin and lay their eggs. If untreated the fur begins to fall out and the skin becomes very dry. The attack usually begins on the head. Treatment should always be supervised by a veterinarian. Canker is caused by a different kind of mite infestation in the ears. Scratching and head shaking will be accompanied by a brownish effusion in the ears and an unpleasant smell. The effusion may

Contrary to general belief many cats know how to swim and some actively enjoy it. Many rex-coated cats seem happy in water and Van cats **(left)** are strong swimmers. One of Colette's cats **(above)** watches as she corrects a manuscript.

Cats like to look down on the rest of the world and
seem unable to resist a pair of step-ladders.
Kittens can sometimes be too adventurous and
mother is wise to keep an eye on her acrobatic
offspring. Owners should be watchful too,
especially when mother is not around.

be removed by gently wiping with a piece of cotton or a stick and applying daily a canker powder or canker drops containing a mite-killing agent. Cats' ears are very delicate organs and need very careful handling. If the infestation seems serious consult your vet, for it can cause other ear conditions.

There are several kinds of worms that can infest cats. Most common are roundworms which are often picked up when very young, or even before birth. Symptoms include slow growth, distended belly and vomiting. The worms, which look like thin pieces of string, may sometimes be seen in the vomit or stool. Your vet can prescribe effective tablet treatment which will clear them. Tapeworms will produce general debility, rejection of food, mild diarrhea and bad temper. If they are passed out with the feces they break up into segments looking like grains of rice. Again, your vet will prescribe an appropriate drug. To ensure correct identification take a feces sample to him.

In some areas, particularly the Pacific Coast states, there is a tiny worm which infests the eye. These are easily removed by your veterinarian but the cat must be anesthetised and tranquilised so never attempt to remove them yourself.

There are other kinds of worms which can attack your pet but they are not so easily recognised. Sickness, diarrhea and other symptoms will alert you that something is wrong.

Ringworm is not a worm but a fungus growth which shows itself as a ring-like patch because the hair roots are affected and the hair breaks off. The usual areas attacked are the ears, face, neck and tail. There are several kinds of ringworm and most of them give off fluorescence under ultra-violet light, but since other substances do this too it needs to be corroborated by other evidence. Since ringworm is spread by tiny spores it is extremely contagious. Complete disinfection of the cat's home should be carried out to ensure that the infection does not spread to other animals or humans.

Cats enjoy climbing trees but they sometimes get themselves into a position from which they have to be rescued.
Left: Poet Robert Graves and his wife feed the cats at their home on Majorca.

Other Ailments

Constipation and diarrhea may be caused by faulty diet. Constipation may be caused by a hairball blockage and this can be serious (see page 103). It can be avoided by giving a little mineral oil on the first signs, and by making sure there is always grass available and plenty of roughage in the diet. In adult cats milk sometimes causes diarrhea. Your cat may have been stealing some unsuitable food. I thought something was seriously wrong with one of my cats until I discovered a bowl of cooking fat had been licked clean! A little kaolin powder mixed with its usual food will usually put your cat right. Both conditions can be an indication of more serious disorders.

Cystitis is an acute inflammation of the bladder. It is an infection that is sometimes complicated by the formation of 'stones' of mineral particles which block the urinary passages. It is extremely painful for the cat which will soon look debilitated. I have known it occur in a mild form in a female on heat for the first time, causing a perfectly house-trained pet to urinate in small amounts in unlikely places because she was unable to control herself, and found it difficult to urinate when she wished to. In a male vomiting may occur and it may lick its penis to ease the pain. Pressure may make it cry out in pain. An early sign is an obvious squatting on the toilet tray. Many owners take cats with this condition to their vets thinking they are constipated. Your veterinarian will be able to treat cystitis with drugs and will either dissolve any stone that has been formed or remove it surgically. In males, particularly, it is essential that veterinary attention is given quickly.

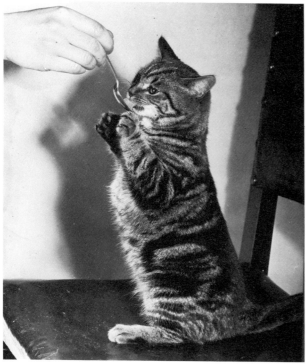

Some cats seem to realize that medicine is to do them good, but if they reject it from a spoon you may have to resort to a plastic syringe or dropper. Like children, cats may be more cooperative if they know a treat will follow.

Pills and Medicines

A cat won't take medication on its own—except for the instinctive kind, like eating grass. Sometimes you can give your pet drugs in powder form sprinkled over food or crumbled into it, but if the cat is off its food or takes a strong dislike to the taste it may not eat enough to make up a proper dosage. If you have more than one pet the wrong one might get the medication, particularly if it decides it likes the taste. One of mine once developed a liking for powder being given for the other's stomach condition, and has a passion for mineral oil, while the other will put up a ceaseless fight to avoid swallowing a drop!

You can simply open the mouths of some cats and pop a spoonful of medication down their throats, or if it is something to which they have taken a liking they may lap it from the spoon—although if they then splash it all over the place they may not take the full dose. To open the mouth hold the cat in your arms, cradling the head in the crook of one arm, then keeping the cat resting stomach up on your lap hold its entire head with one hand gripping the sides of the mouth from behind. With the other hand gently push the lower jaw open, at the same time applying a little pressure either side of the mouth. If this serves to keep the mouth open you can pour the pre-measured medication in with your free hand; if the cat promptly shuts its mouth you may need a helper to give the medicine. Even easier, and safer in that it will ensure that you do not accidentally pour medication down the cat's windpipe, is to use a plastic syringe or dropper. Do not tilt the cat back but, in an upright position, pull a little of the loose skin at the corner of the mouth away from the teeth so that it forms a small pouch, and empty the contents of the syringe into this. To give a pill use the 'head back' method, hold the pill in the hand you use to push the jaw open and place the pill as far back on the tongue as you can.

To make sure the cat swallows the medication hold the mouth shut for a few moments and stroke the neck downwards. You may find that a cat will retain a pill in its mouth for several minutes, pretending to have swallowed it, and will spit it out as soon as it is free. Then you must try again, placing the pill further back so that the cat cannot stop it going down. If you have to administer a course of pills try playing the cat's favorite game immediately after administering the dose and you may be able to get the cat to be cooperative in anticipation of the treat. Obviously if the cat is really sick it probably won't feel like games at all.

If your cat puts up a fight you will find it safer to wrap it in a towel so that you are protected from its claws but you can only avoid its sharp teeth by making sure its mouth stays *open*. Cats are very strong so be prepared for spirited resistance, particularly if the animal is frightened. Under no circumstances give cats drugs of the aspirin group. Salicylates are poisonous to them.

Accidents and Injuries

Cuts, scratches and bites should be carefully cleaned with mild soap and water or a suitable germicidal soap, then give a second cleaning with a weak peroxide solution. The antiseptic liquids made for humans may be used if heavily diluted; some weaker forms are marketed specially for pets. If a cut is deep or very extensive it is advisable to take the cat to the vet for treatment for if all the dirt is not removed an abscess may develop. Cats' wounds heal very rapidly and can easily heal over dirt. If the cat is long-haired you will probably need to trim the hair around the wound to enable you to clean it properly and even with short-haired cats this will be necessary if the wound is serious.

Allow the wound to bleed freely to clear the dirt but if bleeding continues, as may happen with a paw cut on broken glass, apply a tourniquet. Take a pencil and a clean handkerchief. Tie the handkerchief loosely around the leg either just above or below the ankle, slip the pencil through the loop and twist it until the handkerchief is tight enough to stop the flow of blood. Release the pressure every five or ten minutes and tighten again until the flow stops permanently.

However clever you may be at bandaging a human you may find it impossible to keep a bandage on an animal for more than a few minutes. If your cat requires bandaging watch how the vet does it very carefully so that you can change dressings if that is necessary. Bandages on the feet, whether for a foot injury or to prevent the cat scratching itself elsewhere, are particularly difficult but this can be solved by using one of the tubular gauze bandages used for covering fingers. Apply this on top of the ordinary dressing and fix the top with a little adhesive tape.

If you suspect a cat has broken or fractured a bone get the animal to the veterinarian as soon as possible, but to prevent further damage apply a splint to the entire limb. Any firm straight object will do—a ruler for instance. Tie the splint to the bone above and below the suspected fracture and then bandage the whole limb and splint together.

If you suspect broken ribs keep the cat lying down with the broken ribs uppermost.

In the unlikely event of a cat drowning or receiving an electric shock it may be necessary to give artificial respiration. In the case of electric shock you must, of course, switch off the current before touching the cat. Place the cat on the ground and kneel beside it. First make sure that its tongue is pulled to the side of its mouth, then press gently but firmly on the cat's side just behind the shoulder. Relax the pressure and press again at two- or three-second intervals. You may have to keep this up for twenty minutes before breathing is restored.

Shock

Like human beings cats suffering any serious accident or injury are likely to be in shock. The symptoms are a general apathy, breathing in short shallow gasps, a lowering of temperature and possibly spontaneous vomiting or excretion. A cat of nervous temperament may urinate even if only mildly frightened—for instance on being caught and spanked for doing something it knows to be naughty. Treat shock by keeping the animal warm and gently stroking and comforting it until a veterinarian can give more complex treatment.

Poisons

Naturally, you will keep all poisons out of the reach of a cat but you cannot prevent it accidentally eating something poisonous outside the house. If you know that a cat has taken a specific poison left about by accident inform the veterinarian by telephone and ask what antidote to administer. He will probably be able to suggest something made up of household ingredients. If vomiting, panting, trembling, slime dribbling from the mouth, or any other symptoms, make you think your cat may have been poisoned describe them very carefully. The antidote for one poison may be the worst treatment for another. Do not take the animal to the veterinarian since speed is of the utmost importance in administering a remedy.

"Hey diddle-diddle
The Cat and the Fiddle
The Cow jumped over the Moon . . ."
An illustration of the old nursery rhyme.

Birth

Female cats mature more rapidly than males and come 'on heat' for the first time when they are from five to eight months old. Males are not usually sexually mature until they are a year old and sometimes as late as eighteen months. It is not difficult to recognise when a female is on heat. She becomes extremely affectionate, rubbing herself against humans, furniture—anything. She likes being petted and tickled, rolls on her back, and will present herself in positions which would facilitate copulation. She will make different sounds from her usual calls: they may begin as soft crooning murmurs, but as her urge to intercourse develops may rise to a loud howl.

The female can mate only when in season and most cats come on heat at least twice a year, usually in spring and summer, but some cats do come on heat at other times and with a frequency that can be surprising. Many cats call every four or five weeks during spring and summer and some seem never to stop until they have been mated. It is not advisable for a cat to have more than two litters a year. A hormone can be administered which will suppress the oestral cycle if the cat's behavior becomes unbearable—as for instance with the extended calling of a Siamese. This should only be used if you wish to breed the cat but for some reason wish to delay mating.

If you do not wish to breed the cat it should be spayed. This is a simple operation which can be carried out even if your cat has already carried kittens, before she starts her next oestral cycle. It involves an abdominal incision and the removal of the ovaries and uterus. Your pet will have to be left with the vet overnight and later taken back for a few stitches to be removed. It will take a little time for the fur to grow again over the operation scar but the cat will not be affected except in its sexual behavior. A female can be neutered as a kitten or an adult but if you do not want your cat to bear a litter it is advisable to have it done as early as your veterinarian considers suitable.

Neutering a male is an even simpler matter. If carried out on a kitten it does not even require anaesthetic, though one is usually given. Ask your veterinarian to fix an appointment when you take the new kitten to his office for its shots against feline enteritis and pneumonitis.

The first sign of pregnancy is a reddening of the nipples which occurs about three weeks after mating. Soon it becomes clear that the cat is carrying kittens **(above)**. Gestation usually lasts nine weeks from conception.

If your cat runs free it will choose its own mate or mates (it is perfectly possible for kittens in the same litter to have different fathers), but if you have a pedigree cat or one which stays under your control it will be up to you to choose a mate that will be compatible. If you want pedigree kittens you should choose a male who has good points to correct any faults in your female, and you must check both pedigrees to make sure that they are not too closely related. The owner of the stud will expect a fee. Arrangements must be made in advance for the female to be taken or sent to the stud when she is next on heat and when she begins to call the arrangement should be confirmed. When the cat is ready for mating she will exhibit the behavior described above, and the vulva will become noticeably swollen. This condition lasts from four to seven days.

Courtship and mating do not follow a fixed pattern. It may be short or extended, romantic and gentle or violently passionate. After copulation the female pulls herself away from the male with a loud cry and turns on him aggressively. The male cat's penis has barbed projections and it is believed that injury caused by them on withdrawal is the reason for this cry of apparent pain. In some way not yet understood this plays a part in fertilisation.

In her book, *The Natural History of Cats*, Claire Necker quotes a charming folk story to explain this strange behavior. Once upon a time a cat was most put out when in the middle of lovemaking her tom deserted her to chase a mouse. 'She swore that it would never happen again. To prevent it she screamed at intervals during future amours thereby scaring the mice and keeping them at a distance. This expedient proved so successful that all female cats have continued to do it to this very day.'

Most stud owners will see that the queen receives two matings before returning her and many will allow a further visit without charge if conception does not result. In case the mating has not been successful it is advisable to keep the cat away from other males for at least a week after her return.

There will be no immediate signs of pregnancy but after about three weeks the nipples may become slightly reddened and after a month they will begin to swell. By this time a veterinarian will be able to confirm pregnancy by feeling the internal development. The cat will behave normally and should be treated as usual except that a little additional calcium should be added to the diet and the amount of food increased as the cat demands it. Vitamin and mineral supplement may also be given.

The period of gestation is usually 63–65 days (kittens born before the sixtieth day rarely survive) but some cats may not kitten until as late as 70 days after conception. Many cats like to have their owners near at hand when they give birth and are able to delay their kittening if they are not available. Toward the end of pregnancy the cat will grow increasingly careful and will begin to look for a place to have her kittens. This is the time to prepare a large box lined with plenty of clean newspaper. The sides must be low enough for the queen to see over from outside and to get in and out without difficulty. Put it in a dark, quiet, draught-free corner or a cupboard, where the cat can feel secure and away from interference. She will tear up the newspaper to make a nest. When you think that she is ready to give birth, of which the signs are milk in the nipples, calling, restlessness and sometimes a discharge from an increasingly distended vulva, cover the newspaper with a blanket to keep the kittens warm and an old towel to keep the blanket clean. Your cat may decide to have her kittens somewhere quite different but you will see her preparing a place and can transfer the box to suit her choice.

126

Most queens, even with a first litter, manage the whole thing without any help, biting the umbilical cords, eating the placenta and cleaning the kittens. If you are allowed to be present, after each delivery make a note that the afterbirth is eaten or removed for if one should be retained within the cat it could lead to serious infection. If there is any chance of a natural birth proving difficult a caesarean section may be recommended. This is carried out in a similar way as for a human caesarean birth. Your veterinarian will be able to predict any likely difficulties and instruct you on how to deal with them. Most cat births, however, are straightforward and need no human help. The kittens should be sexed as soon as possible and any unwanted ones taken to the veterinarian to be painlessly destroyed.

The kittens can begin to suck from thirty minutes after birth but may wait as much as two hours and often they will not be allowed to suckle until all the litter has been delivered. In a household with more than one female cat the others may act as midwives and will probably help in rearing and training the kittens, but they will know their own mother.

Watching a cat raise its litter, caring for them, disciplining them, and teaching them, can be a fascinating experience. Sometimes, as a mother cat carries a kitten in her teeth, holding it by the loose skin at the back of the neck, with the little thing curling up to try to avoid bumps as it bounces along the floor you may think that she is being very rough but in almost every case she instinctively knows best. Occasionally when there is only one kitten in a litter the mother seems to lose interest, but bad mothers are extremely rare.

Most cats can cope with motherhood without any difficulty but you should know how to help in case problems do arise. The cat **(above left and above)** is cleaning a new-born kitten. The litter **(left)** is several weeks old.

127

Six Senses and Nine Lives

Physiologically the cat is not so very different from man. It has a very similar skeleton and all the same organs but the cat is much more lithe and can stretch and arch its back. The cat's shoulder joint enables it to turn its foreleg in any direction and it has a very small collarbone—sometimes none at all—which makes movement more free. It lacks such versatile fingers and has only a rudimentary thumb; it has retractile claws instead of static nails and in its hind-quarters the foot is used as part of the leg and it walks only on its toes. It also walks on four feet instead of balancing on two. With the exception of the Manx cat it has retained its tail.

Their equipment is like our own but they have to rely upon it far more than we do and it is therefore much more carefully refined and precisely controlled. For its size the cat is also remarkably strong, as you will soon discover if you hold a cat that wants to struggle free or see a cat administer a hard blow with its paws. However, a cat cannot keep going for long periods—short bursts of energy are the pattern, interspersed with rests and 'naps'. This is because it has a small chest cavity and consequently small lungs and heart. Its digestive organs are correspondingly large to allow it to gorge itself and then go without food until it can catch another meal.

Sight

Cats, with man and the monkey family, are the only mammals which rely on sight rather than smell (though they still use smell to locate food at short range, *see below*). They have an extremely sensitive optical system which is far more efficient than our own. Their angle of view for each eye is over 200° and although the eyes are placed forward so that the fields of vision overlap they are able to turn their heads so easily that this is no handicap. Their pupils dilate and contract from a full circle in the dark to a barely visible slit in bright light. Pupil reflex and focus adjustment are very swift which help in judging distances. To see things in three dimensions it is necessary for nerve fibers which have received the same image to reach each side of the brain from both eyes. In normal cats about half the nerve fibers make connexions on the opposite side of the brain to the eye. Research at the Massachusetts Institute of Technology has suggested that in the Siamese *all* the connexions cross over, canceling the effect out and making it impossible to see stereoscopically. Since Siamese seem to be as adept as any other breed at jumping accurately this would emphasise the efficiency of their optical system

and the speed of their response to the two-dimensional information it brings. Nevertheless, it seems amazing that a cat could spring over the distances I have observed and make an accurate landing without being able to see in depth.

It used to be thought that cats did not see in color. This is now known to be untrue but compared with man they have about six times the proportion of retinal rods (which react to light intensity) to retinal cones (which register color). The ratio for cats is about 20–25:1 which gives them excellent vision for night hunting. The cat also has a layer of reflecting cells called the *tapetum lucidum* which intensifies the light by reflecting any that has not been absorbed in its passage through the eye back onto the retinal cells. This gives amazing brightness discrimination—seven times better than our own—which enables it to see light long after we consider ourselves in pitch darkness. Of course, there must be some light; no eye, however sensitive, can see in absolute darkness. It is the *tapetum lucidum* reflecting available light which makes a cat's eyes apparently shine in the dark and which causes the eyes of Siamese to look red when they catch the light.

A cat will patiently watch its prey (or a piece of string) with a concentration which seems unbroken, and which can seem decidedly accusing when turned upon oneself. This ability is part of its hunting equipment for it is watching for movement rather than shape. However, a domestic cat rapidly learns to identify shape if it is encouraged to do so.

The cat has an extra eyelid, the *nictitating membrane*, which closes sideways and upward from the inner corner of the eye. It is partly transparent and protects the cat's eyes from damage in a fight or when pushing through rough undergrowth; it also cuts down the intensity of over-bright light. If it is permanently closed or partly closed it is a sign of sickness or damage to the eye.

Smell

The cat enjoys smells and will vigorously investigate all those picked up in a day on its owner's clothes, or another cat's fur, or wafting through an open window, in addition to those more solidly available. Most cats are passionately attracted to the smell of the plants catnip and valerian, and also like many other herbs and plants. They like man-made perfumes and interesting cooking smells but they will equally savor smells which we would find unpleasant.

A cat's main practical use of the sense of smell is to locate food. Having fixed location visually it seems to shut off the evidence of its eyes and will sniff within inches of a piece of meat before finding it. Smell also plays a vital part in the sex life of the cat. Each cat announces its sex through its own smell and male cats can sense a female on heat at a great distance.

The nose is sensitive but once a scent has been registered the cat will sniff to intensify the smells it wishes to investigate and will often open its mouth also to intensify the sensation in a way we do not yet understand. The nostrils are equipped both to filter the air and to warm it. A healthy cat will usually have a cold wet nose.

Hearing

A cat's ears are shaped and lined with ridges to collect and concentrate sound. They can move backward and forward, upward and downward; and a cat's neck is so flexible that it can be turned to catch and locate a sound from any direction. Their range of hearing is very wide— from 30,000 to 45,000 cycles per second, only beginning to fall off during the top 5,000 cycles. Man's optimum range is from 2,000 to 4,000 cycles but even in that range a cat hears better than we do. Its optimum range extends to 8,000 cycles. The organ of balance, the semicircular canals of the inner ear are also extremely sensitive.

Cats can distinguish and recognise sounds with great facility. Its owner's step or the sound of a car engine will be identified from all the others passing in the street and the difference between important human words, particularly names, is soon recognised.

Watch a cat carefully when you are holding a conversation with it and you will see that it is using its ears to talk to you. You may not be able to provide an accurate translation of the small movements and twitches but anyone who has ever owned a cat will know that they press their ears downward to protect them and to provide a less prominent profile before they make an attack, that they lay them back against the head to look more savage, and at a slightly different angle if they are apprehensive, especially if expecting punishment for a misdemeanor. Upright they suggest a happy lively awareness, pricked forward an intense interest and concentration.

All the cat's senses, except perhaps that of smell, are highly developed. There is not much that escapes a cat's attention.

132

Speech

The cat's voice can range from a low purr to a sharp harsh cry with all manner of hisses, growls, puffs and huffs. The Siamese and similar breeds have a stronger, harsher voice which some people find unpleasant. Certainly a Siamese female on heat produces a call whose repetition is difficult to bear.

A mother cat will chirp and chortle to her kittens using sounds not heard at other times except from kittens who have not learned an adult vocabulary. It is a language of which human beings only master a few sounds: cats are much better at understanding human talk.

Cats make some apparently involuntary sounds. When excited by noticing a fly, bird or other prey, or irritated by its inaccessibility, they often make a chattering like a machine-gun with their teeth. When they are really contented they will usually purr. Exactly *how* they purr is still not properly understood. Some cats purr silently—or at least so that humans cannot hear them although they can feel the vibrations, others purr so loudly they sound like a giant machine—and demonstrate their contentment sitting on one's pillow when you are trying to get to sleep! Sometimes cats make a slightly different purr when they are in pain. This is a subject about which a great deal remains to be discovered.

There are many proprietary pet foods available for cats, but you may have to try several brands before you can find one which your cat will like, and it may reject them all. You should certainly not give your cat a diet consisting entirely of canned food — however "enriched with added vitamins". Your cat will prefer variety and will be healthier for a carefully chosen balanced diet.

Taste

A cat senses taste largely through its tongue although there are also a few taste buds on the soft palate and surrounding areas of the mouth. Adult cats are not very sensitive to sweet things, fairly sensitive to salt or bitter tastes, and most to sour. It was once considered that their sense of taste was negligible but this seems to be denied by the marked preference individual cats show for certain foods. It is possible that texture and smell play a large part in their choice. Taste does not seem to play a practical role in their survival as wild animals.

Touch

A cat's whole body is hypersensitive to touch. Something brushing against one hair of the head or back can provoke a response. This ultra-sensitivity is due to small, slightly raised areas known as touch spots or, more technically, tylotrich pads which are depressed if a single hair is moved, sending an immediate signal to the cat's nervous system.

Touch is one of its most important senses. In the dark it will supplement its already highly sensitive eyes and in real darkness it replaces sight. It is one of the primary ways of investigating new objects and materials. The investigation may be carried out with the nose and the tongue, both of which are highly attuned to touch, but more particularly, with its paws. Quite a large part of the brain is devoted to the sense of touch from the forepaws alone, which gives some indication of their importance. Both as a tiny kitten and an adult cat they will be used to explore texture, size and shape. Although a cat cannot hold things in its 'fingers' it can cup its paws and hold onto objects and if it is sure they will not be harmed, or it considers that an unnecessary consideration, it will grip with its claws. But how rarely a cat will fail to retract its claws, however fully they have been extended a moment before, if landing on naked skin.

In addition to these touch organs the cat has a set of sensors known as vibrissae: the whiskers, eyebrows, other cheek hairs and the long hairs on the wrists of the front legs, which are all hairs modified to turn them into ultra-sensitive organs of touch. They respond not only to direct contact and to obvious currents of air, but also to those minute changes of air pressure and movement caused by the presence of objects.

It is an old wives' tale that a cat's whiskers grow to its width so that it can tell whether it can get through a hole or not—but it does use them to evaluate the size of the hole, and a cat with damaged or missing whiskers will exhibit bad spatial judgment.

Cats use touch as a means of communication. When they are excited their whiskers bristle. When they are affectionate they rub with their nose and lick, sometimes even giving human friends a thorough wash.

A Sixth Sense?

Cats often seem to be aware of things that pass their owners unnoticed. A cat will suddenly bristle, its tail go into the bush 'Christmas tree' that indicates aggression or fear, and it will stare fixedly at—nothing. Does it see a ghost?

There are many stories of cats who having been moved from one home to another find their way back to their old and preferred territory. Although this may suggest remarkable ability, cats are territorial animals and it is possible to produce some kind of explanation, for at least the cat knows the conditions, the relationship to the sun and so forth of the place it left behind. What are truly remarkable are the authenticated instances of cats who have found their way not to an old haunt but, having been left there, have set out and found their way to a family or owner who has moved away.

When a cat is concentrating on its prey if often makes an excited chattering noise like a small machine-gun. It is not known why, for surely it gives warning to the creature it is hoping to catch.

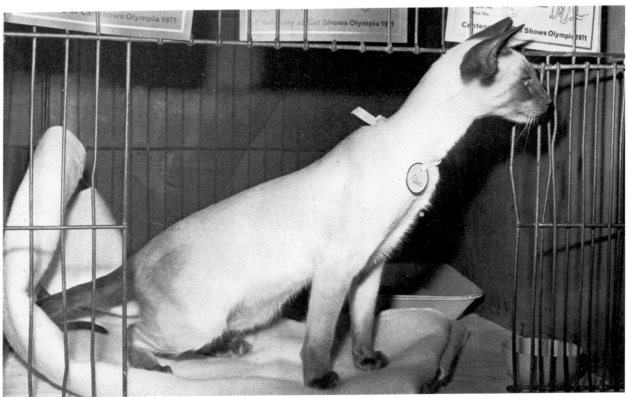

Take just three cases. One cat who refused to leave when a family moved from California to Oklahoma turned up fourteen months later in their new home. Of course, he may have waited for an opportunity to recognise their writing on a letter written to neighbors, memorised the new address and booked himself onto a Greyhound bus . . . hardly less likely than any other explanation! Another cat found its way 294 miles from Louisiana to Texas. A cat belonging to a New York veterinarian which had to be left behind when he took up a post in California turned up at the new address five months later having traveled at least 2,300 miles. It would be easy to suggest that these were all cats that just looked like the ones left behind but in all cases they not only looked and behaved alike and recognised their humans but each had a physical deformity which made their identity unquestionable.

For centuries sailors believed that cats could see a storm coming and there are many claims that cats have behaved with foreknowledge of earthquake. Both of those are natural phenomena and there may be instinctive reaction to changes of temperature and pressure, but how can one explain the apparent anticipation of air raids shown by some cats or their foreknowledge of the return of someone who is not expected—not simply by hearing or scenting their arrival but by behaving well in advance as though they anticipate it.

How, too, can one explain the cat's uncanny sense of time? House pets recognise the normal weekly pattern—cats who make a habit of waking their owners up will know when it is the weekend and there is no hurry to be up and off to work. They probably recognise a difference in the way their owners sleep. But how can one explain how cats recognise a time pattern related to people or events outside their own household?

Perhaps the ancient Egyptians and the medieval believers in the supernatural were reacting to forces which must baffle even the sceptics of today.

Nine Lives

A cat seems to be born with so much instinctive knowledge about prey, about herbs and about itself, and to learn so easily in a way that seems more like revision, that it is tempting to think that it is recollecting the experience of former incarnations, but as the cat Tobermory says in Saki's splendid tale, 'I may have nine lives, but I only have one liver.'

No, the cat's apparent power over death comes more from the number of narrow escapes it survives, the number of situations which would have spelt the end of any other creature. The cat's well-organised musculature, flexible skeleton and superb control, aided by sharp claws and well-armed jaws, equip it to survive both accident and battle, falling victim only to disease, exhaustion, poison, the motor car—and their own carelessness.

Despite tradition, even water does not necessarily hold any fears. Although most cats, like us, do not like to get wet accidentally, some are accomplished fishermen, almost all instinctively know how to swim and a few actively enjoy it. How many other animals would survive the ordeal which Captain John Locke described on a trip from Venice to Jerusalem in 1589:

It chanced by fortune that the shippes Cat lept into the sea, which being downe, kept her selfe very valiantly above water, notwithstanding the great waves, still swimming, the which the master knowing, he caused the Skiffe with halfe a dozen men to goe towards her and fetch her againe, when she was almost halfe a mile from the shippe. . . . I hardly believe they would have made such haste and means if one of the company had bene in the like perill. They made the more haste because it was the patron's cat. This I have written onely to note the estimation that cats are in, among the Italians, for generally they esteeme their cattes, as in England we esteeme a good Spaniell.

Falling on its Feet

Singular among the cat's accomplishments, and one which must have saved its life on many occasions, is its ability to land on its feet. Some other animals share this righting capacity but not to the same degree. Experiment and careful observation has shown that this is not the result of any pattern of movement initiated on take-off—as for instance are the gyrations of a fancy diver. The cat is actually able to turn itself *while falling*. While falling there is nothing against which the cat can push itself to adjust its angle; it has to turn by twisting one part of the body against the rest. Different cats use different methods of achieving this according to their build and skill—but do it they can from the time that they can run. They cannot however right themselves if dropped in a completely vertical position for the body cannot then twist

Cats have accurate judgement of distances and very fast reactions so that they can rapidly adjust when, for instance, they jump upon a surface that is above their line of sight. Nevertheless they can be careless. This cat's owner (**left**) has allowed a potentially dangerous situation. The hot iron could easily fall.

A cat twists and begins to right itself as soon as it starts to fall. The nerves which convey information about movement from the body surface and the labyrinth, or inner ear, which is linked with balance, contribute to this "righting reflex" which is already present in the unborn kitten.

against the plane of the fall. Righting themselves is not the whole job. They have to land safely too. With their back arched and all four legs extended they cushion their landing without serious harm. What they cannot control is the speed with which they fall, which depends on their size and weight.

The British scientist Donald McDonald has carried out experiments which suggest that from a height of about sixty feet or more the resistance of the air balances out the acceleration of the fall. Since cats have fallen safely from trees of this height there is no reason why height should present any problem. At the opposite extreme, although they turn very rapidly, they might not be able to right themselves if dropped awkwardly by a small child less than three feet from the ground. A man falling fifty feet would usually be killed so, understandably, Mr McDonald published his findings (*New Scientist,* 30 June 1960) without carrying out that experiment with a real cat, but he did experiment (from low heights and using a rubber mattress as a landing ground) with a fifteen-year-old cat belonging to Professor Haldane which was deaf. He found that it was still able to right itself but when blindfolded was not only unable to do so during the fall but was very slow in doing so even after it had landed on the mattress. It had previously been believed that the ears, which are closely related to the sense of balance, played the major part in controling the cat's maneuver. It is not possible that this cat had gained experience in its youth and was able to adjust as it became deaf for it was born so. Hence sight on its own can provide enough of the necessary information. No doubt its full faculties are brought into play if they are present, but exactly how still remains a mystery. What we can be sure of is that sight establishes the relationship to the horizon while parts of the ear sense the position of the head and register rotation.

Dreams

Like us cats seem to have another life when they are asleep: from about ten days old a cat begins to dream. What they dream, and whether dreams play the same role as they do in human beings we cannot know, but from their reactions whilst asleep it is clear that they can have happy dreams, which make them purr with pleasure, and agitated dreams—nightmares perhaps?—in which they tremble and flex their claws.

Life Expectancy

Medical research has increased animal life expectancy as much as it has helped humans to live longer. Perhaps cats are the luckier for if they are healthy they can enjoy a happy old age and if they are in great pain they will not be expected to bear it indefinitely whilst being pumped with drugs in a geriatric ward. Their life expectancy has now been increased from about twelve years to fifteen or even seventeen years for a cat which has been kept in good condition. One cat in Los Angeles lived to be thirty-three. It is impossible to compare a cat's age with the human scale. You cannot call four months a cat's year, or use any comparative measure, for a cat leaves its mother after only a few weeks and achieves adulthood in a year or eighteen months. A human being achieves physical independence only after several years, is sexually mature in its teens and not a fully responsible independent adult until after a cat's natural life has ended. However in a happy home they can retain their vitality and youthful character far longer than you or me, and remain a pleasant companion until the last.